Wolf Song

First Edition

Library of Congress Cataloging-in-Publication Data

Spencer, Jeanette.
Wolf Song Cards: The Book/by Jeanette Spencer and Lew Hartman.

p. cm.

Includes bibliographical references (p.).

ISBN 1-57281-256-7

1. Tarot. 2. Animals—Miscellanea. I. Hartman, Lew. II. Title.

BF1879.T2 S72 2000

133.3'242—dc21

00 10 9 8 7 6 5 4 3 2 1

Printed in Canada

U.S. Games Systems, Inc.
179 Ludlow Street
Stamford, CT 06902 USA

Dedicated to my parents, Thomas L. and Rosmarie M. Spencer, each of whom loves animals not only as people of other tribes, but as thinking, feeling individuals. They taught me, by their words and deeds, that man has stewardship, not dominion over animals.

Special thanks to Kenneth B. Dowling, President, Florida Technical College. Thank you for the generous gifts of you help, your advice, and your faith in me.

Thank you, Dana Duncan O'Kelly, Editor, U.S. Games Systems, Inc., for your professionalism and your unfailing good humor.

—*Jeanette Spencer*

I want to dedicate *Wolf Song* to my Uncle Lew who inspired my love of nature and animals, and to my wife, Kathy Hartman and my son, Lewis John Hartman VII.

—*Lewis John Hartman VI*

Together, we dedicate *Wolf Song* to all the animals who are, who have been, and who will be.

Wolf Song

BY
JEANETTE SPENCER
AND
LEW HARTMAN

U.S. GAMES
SYSTEMS, INC

Published by
U.S. GAMES SYSTEMS, INC.
Stamford, CT 06902 USA

Preface

Wolf Song sprang from the fertile mind of Lew Hartman after a conversation with Stuart Kaplan of U.S. Games. It was not a little idea that occurred to him, but a great one of full fruit borne of years of intense study of art, letters, and animals. The Wolf Song deck is not just the sixty stunning paintings, but a love of animals, a concern for people, and the acknowledgment of change in our lives.

Many changes took place as Wolf Song evolved from a concept to a concrete form. One of the changes was that Hartman decided not to write the companion book, but to contact another artist, one who was also a writer, fond of animals, and as interested in their behavior as he.

Lew and I met because of a Florida Panther in the care of Bert Wahl, head of Wildlife Rescue, Tampa. A magnificent male, the Panther has a name in his own language, and is an ambassador who represents his tribe to our kind so that we may understand the precious and fragile nature of their lives. Lew is second to none in the donation of his time and beautiful art work to Wildlife Rescue for care of the many Panthers and other captive wildlife in their custody.

Over the years, I have often written on subjects concerning animals, wild and domestic. It has been my privilege to interview experts in the field of Native American wildlife as well as work with experts such as Bert Wahl and Cyndi Westra of Save the Wildlife, Orlando. I have been fortunate enough to be included in the "family" of Faith, a female Florida Panther in Cyndi's care. When Cyndi told me that another artist was contributing artwork to raise funds for Faith, our other animals, and the companion animal hospice, I was thrilled. When she showed me a sketch, I immediately recognized it as Lew's work.

However, it was not yet time for me to be included in

the Wolf Song project. I was to be lucky enough to serve on a Native American publication, Pow Wow Trails, and to write about ethnological and animal subjects. I was also teaching Art and Art History as a professor at Florida Technical College. Life seemed to be quite complete.

I was wrong; life was only waiting to drop a wonderful change into my path. In part, the opportunity came because of the love and respect Lew and I share for animals. Another factor was our shared graduate history (Lew studied English, I studied History; we both studied Art and Mythology). However, the final element in the change was something that happened in my life, by chance, when I was a teenager.

Being a professor, an artist, a writer, and a lover of animals were not the reasons I was chosen. The reason is that I have been a tarot reader since I was fifteen. My first book was *Tarot Cards for Fun and Fortune Telling*, written by Stuart Kaplan and published by U.S. Games Systems, Inc. The book was a gift from a friend along with a Rider-Waite tarot deck. That I could do the research, that I can write and have a long history of published work, that I am an artist who also draws and paints animals, and that I am an academic, all paled when compared to the fact I am a tarot reader.

Because I am a reader of tarot, as well as palms and crystals, I can tell you that the greatest strength of Wolf Song is not predicting the future, but helping you see the present (and the past that has made this present), and shape your future as you please. Yes, you can use it as a tarot deck, but do not overlook its greatest gift.

When Brother Wolf looked out over the land and saw the puny, frightened humans living lonely, hard lives, he taught them how to live as a pack. He taught them to have a sense of self and of community, and he gave us the great gift of the clan. Each animal has given us a great gift, as did the Wolf, and now each gives us the greatest gift of all—the knowledge of self.

The changes in the lives of Lew and myself came as a gift from the animals, and from the legends and lore of our ancestors, regardless of their color or geographic location. Listen to the song of the words, see the feast before your eyes, and learn. To know yourself is to understand. And understanding is the key to all things.

—Jeanette Spencer

Introduction

The Essence of the Wolf Song Cards is change. The premise of the deck is that Life's only constant force is change. Change, whether day to night, season to season, or even standard to daylight-saving time, pervades everything we do, wish, and dream. The achievement of any goal is also a function of change.

All people are united by the same forces. We are all of the earth, brothers and sisters to one another and to the people of other tribes. Each tribe has its spirit, and our ancestors petitioned the spirits of all tribes for succor, comfort, and knowledge. Wisdom has always been understanding how little each of us really knows. True wisdom is seeking to learn, seeking greater awareness.

In this deck, homage is paid to many tribes of North America. Their animal spirits were acknowledged among the earliest communities of the human family, as the ambassadors of the force uniting all things.

The Wolf has been petitioned as the first among equals in this deck to learn greater awareness. The Spirit of the Wolf was invoked by Native Americans during times of drought and famine. The Wolf embodies the expert hunter who is a valuable, loyal member of a larger community. The Spirit of the Wolf aided in the hunt, representing the skill of the individual and the group. Of most importance, the Spirit of the Wolf filled the empty vessels, symbolizing the importance of the one and the many.

Wolves have always held a preeminent place in human history. Native Americans and Eskimos co-exist with the Wolf tribe, considering them to be fellow hunters and recognizing significant virtues. They admire the individual prowess of the animal and point to the cooperation among members of the pack to ensure the survival of the clan.

Native Americans compare their own societies with that of the Wolf. The hunting parties of each consist of a band of hunters and one or two leaders. Wolves who do not hunt care for the young and guard the den; they share in the bounties brought in by the hunters, just as their human counterparts. It is said among several Indian tribes that they learned the way of the family from the Wolf.

Native Americans and Eskimos never failed to recognize their fellow hunters as predators. They had no romantic notions of wolves. The Wolf is, after all, a practical creature and, like his human fellows, will make sure the pack survives.

The Wolf has never been as bad as many cultures claimed. Some of the blame the wolf shoulders belongs more properly to his accusers. Many a poacher has left the sign of the wolf as he makes off with the King's game or the farmer's sheep. Truth be told, a fair number of farmers have blamed wolves for their own deeds. European and Eastern legends tend to cast the wolf in a bad light. One tale told in Northern Europe speaks of a beautiful woman who arrives during the Winter Solstice celebrations. Each night she comes, a person she favors disappears. Finally, one of two warrior brothers puts himself in a position to be the favored so he can find out what she is. However, he is disarmed and enchanted by her and also disappears.

His brother resolves to find the warrior, and sets out across the snow to find tracks. Ultimately, the younger brother discovers that the beautiful woman is a white wolf, what we now call the Alpha female, who is providing prey to prevent her pack from starving. He saves his brother at the cost of his own life, but is said to haunt the site as a handsome black wolf, the mate of the white wolf. It is probable that the darkly romantic epilogue was added during the gothic period when romance and horror were often entwined.

Compare this with a Native American legend that speaks of a man cast into a pit by two women who hold a grudge against him. He is rescued from the pit by his fellow warriors, two wolves. One is white, the other is described as "rabid"; meaning in this case not the disease but the condition of insanity, thought to be the result of having been touched by the sacred spirit.

During a course of adventures, the white wolf protects the man from the other wolf; both teach him many things. He is escorted to their land and accepted as a member of the pack. Armed with great knowledge, now a Wolf Warrior, he returned to his people. He kills the two women who left him to die, and presents their bodies to the wolves as a gift.

Both legends are dark, both are romantic. But the Native American legend casts the wolves, even one that is rabid, as heroes, whereas the Norse legend condemns them as villains. However, despite the nearly overwhelming tendency in the past to see wolves as vicious, sneaky and ill-mannered (as in the case of the beautiful white wolf who was quite rude to eat members of her host's family), there is the glimmer of recognition of what the Native Americans saw, animals being both noble and redeeming, but most importantly, true to their own spirit.

Remember this: if all else fades before you, be as true to your own best spirit as the wolf is to his nature.

The cunning ask "how?" The wise ask "why?"

Timber Wolf

NATURAL, POSITIVE CHANGE

Time is marked by the passing of seasons and Timber Wolf tells of natural, positive change. Natural change is the way of life. Timber Wolf tells of birth and death, rebirth and growth. He tells us of history made and being made.

The Nation of the Wolf has two main tribes, the Red Wolf and the Gray Wolf. Timber Wolf's tribe was born of the Gray Wolf. The division of the tribe was not preformed in anger or animosity. It was a natural, positive change of circumstance. Since then, Timber Wolf has been the symbol of such change. Timber Wolf honors his family and serves his community. He understands the evolution of family and community. Each generation remains family, but each family member must make his or her own community. After a time, the clan is a tribe, the tribe is a nation, and so life continues.

Timber Wolf comes to counsel you that accepting change is not just a casting off of the old, but an embracing of the new. Your heritage and your history remain yours. What you were is part of what you are and what you will be. He speaks to you of the seasons. As the fruits of summer sustain you during winter, you will take what you know and follow the path to new life.

Remember, Timber Wolf says to you, that your life is not only four seasons long. You have times of rest, times of play, times of great learning. You walk the path of time only in the physical sense. Your psychic self and your spiritual self are no more constrained than your intellect has to be. Hone your senses, learn all that you can.

You must, Timber Wolf tells you, be ready. You cannot stop change. You can ignore it, but at great cost to you and yours. Rather, accept the rule of life that nothing remains the same. Learn, grow, teach and experience all the positives you can in your intellectual, spiritual, physical and psychic life. Do not see change as a new start, but a chance to employ what you have learned and discovered in the past. You will bring your experience with you and create new solutions. Timber Wolf tells you to work to be a problem solver, not a victim of problems. Step forward and accept the role of responsibility. Accept, too, the joy of life. Timber Wolf tells you there must be balance, your life is color, not just pale shades of gray.

Further, you must persevere. Despite all odds, and in spite of all hatreds born of fear and a lack of knowledge, you must survive and you must rise above the obstacles that will be thrown in your path by people who are small and fearful, even jealous. Like the Nation of the

Wolf, you will persevere, but only if you avoid the traps others set before you.

The reverse of this card is a sign of resisting necessary change. Change is the way of life and time, it must be embraced. If not embraced, then endured. Approach each challenge in life with an open mind and humor.

Gray Wolf

NECESSARY CHANGE

Gray Wolf's character is strong and warm. He maintains his dignity, but he is not reluctant to let his feelings be known. He can keep a secret, but he is not secretive. He works hard and he plays hard. His spiritual life is strong and his intellectual life is the core of his being. Gray Wolf's resolve and devotion are legendary for good reason.

In the dim light of early history, it is said that man learned to live in families and then communities after being taught how by the Gray Wolf. He imparted this knowledge in many places, for Gray Wolf is truly a citizen of the world. His tribe dwells in almost every place that human kind also dwells. For his contribution, Gray Wolf is honored most often as an Elder Being, a wise and venerated teacher.

Gray Wolf has a rich history to draw upon, as well as the texture of experience he shares. A loyal mate and devoted parent, Gray Wolf is also an active member of his community. He approaches every task with an eye toward what he can do, rather than wondering who is going to do anything. He pays attention to those around him and he realizes change is a way of life for all living things.

Gray Wolf comes to you to teach that change is necessary. Assail and complain all you will, you will waste your energies. Gray Wolf tells you to apply those energies toward adapting to the changes you must either endure or welcome.

Time is change; for whether we are willing or unwilling, everything changes. Gray Wolf symbolizes the wisdom of accepting that which cannot be changed; ironically, change itself.

Gray Wolf also tells us of the need to make changes. When he comes to you, it is to tell you of the need to make necessary changes. Look deep inside yourself and ask your soul what you need to change about yourself and in your life. Respond to each situation in your environment, do not merely react.

Remember, too, Gray Wolf counsels, that each of us was put here to learn and to teach. We are here to be helped and to help. Our lives are our own, but our lives are also part of the family and the community. We are independent, we are dependent, as well as depended upon. Understand that the texture of experience is multi-layered like the strata of the earth's mantle. Never think it is a single-leveled weave where things proceed and then end. Where have you fallen into the trap of complacency? What are you doing to pull yourself out of the quagmire of no longer caring? Address the issues, be passionate, give your passion to others. Do not substitute the satisfaction of performing necessary chores for the feeling of performing great and wonderful tasks. Strive to make the world a better place, do not waste your energy trying to dominate or control.

Educate and enlighten, do not browbeat or threaten. Extend your hand, do not raise your fist. If you would change the world, Gray Wolf counsels, first change yourself.

The reverse of this card warns us of not accepting the need for change. This is a self-defeating attitude that prevents the growth of your spirit. You must accept change, and you may as well embrace it. You cannot stop it, you can only pretend that it is not so.

Red Wolf

UNEXPECTED CHANGE

Red Wolf is intelligent and quiet. He maintains a reserve that is almost shy. Alert as well as gifted, he is always watching for opportunity. He knows, even more than his fellow wolves, about change and how unexpected it can be. Red Wolf, however, is equal to any challenge change may present. He will take the change and turn it to his advantage whenever possible. If it is not possible, he will endure, using his great spiritual sense to weather any storm. He is a survivor, no matter what the odds. Red Wolf is not as large as other members of the Wolf Nation, but he is equally imposing. He was never, so it is said, a member of the Gray Wolf

Tribe, but a separate tribe. However, some few say Red Wolf is a hybrid between the Coyote and the Gray Wolf. Others argue that he is a true wolf.

But, Red Wolf asks, what is a true wolf? If legends are correct, it is the Coyote who is the father of the wolf clan to begin with. But who is the mother? There are some who say human kind contributed to the birth of the wolf; you can look into his eyes for the proof you need. So then, he asks again, what is a true wolf? Now, Red Wolf says, ask yourself how many truths there really are?

Red Wolf lives the life of a wolf, and that is truth enough. He is devoted to his mate, his children and his community. He is valiant not because he seeks approval, but because the job needs to be done.

Worry less, counsels Red Wolf, about what others think and more about learning how to think for yourself. Depend on no one for the definition of who or what you are. Define yourself, and stand true no matter what changes spill over you like rain in the summer.

Red Wolf urges you to take notice of your environment and understand the impact just one can have. Look and see what life is bringing you every moment. Do not close your eyes.

Remember, unexpected change is not, of itself, negative. It is only change not anticipated or planned. Unexpected change can be the means of achieving your goals; a path previously overlooked. Further analysis and thought may be required. When Red Wolf presents himself, simply be prepared to adapt to the new course of events.

Red Wolf has more counsel, wise and born of experience. There will be times when you will be the center of unexpected change, when you and you alone must manage the swirling tide. This time will arrive, of course, without notice and without expectation. Be prepared to handle the situation. Learn what you can about whatever it is for which you have a talent and an understanding. You cannot be an expert at everything, but you can be an expert at getting the information you need, and approaching the experts for advice. Management is as much digging out information as it is having information. It is as much teaching and learning as it is guiding and leading.

The reverse of this card indicates a fear of change or the unexpected. Stand like Red Wolf, put your fears behind you, and face the challenges. Shed your desire to command every aspect of your environment.

Arctic Wolf

RESISTANCE TO CHANGE

Arctic Wolf is, as are most wolves, reserved. He tends to be even more quiet around those he does not know. He observes others and decides whether they are worth his time before he approaches or allows himself to be approached. He is very business-like, courteous but aloof. He would rather do his job and go home to his family than socialize with those with whom he works.

Arctic Wolf is part of the greater Gray Wolf Tribe. Like Timber Wolf, his clan grew and became another tribe. He shares the Wolf Nation's love of family and community. He prides himself on being a loving mate and a good parent.

He does not fear change. He, like his brothers, understands change. However, he comes not only to tell you of coming change, but the need to manage the course of change.

Living in a clime that is beautiful but unforgiving, Arctic Wolf calls the cold and frozen tundra home. His is the least changing of all environments, and can lead to resistance to that which is new or different. The resistance may come from many directions, including from the Self, but is not always negative. The resistance may be nothing more than asking questions which must be answered to gain the wisdom you seek.

There are changes brought not by life and the Universe, but by you. The question is whether or not you have considered all of the ramifications? Are you prepared to sacrifice what you have and what you are? Ask yourself, "why do I want change?" Am I bored or am I overwhelmed? If I change my environment, is it beneficial?

Arctic Wolf tells you that the attainment of knowledge and experience is to be lauded. However, he counsels, there are experiences that are not worthy of the time and energy you must expend. Is this goal something that will help you grow spiritually? Is it something that will help you develop your intellect? Is this something you will share with your children and your other students? Is it something that you will be proud of having done?

Be wary, as the Arctic Wolf, of changes that occur for no other reason than self- involvement. Change will not solve old problems. Remember that change does not absolve or solve. It merely is and it merely occurs.

If you are running away, nothing good will happen. If you turn your back on the ones who love you, depend upon you and look up to you, no matter how great or small they are, the only change you will experience is one of emptiness. You will destroy all good and you will lose the trust of the Universe as well as your family, friends and community. The loss may not mean much at first, but you will come to realize what you have lost, and nothing will have been worth the cost.

You are a member of a family, a clan, a tribe, a community. You have your rights, and you have your responsibilities. Being the lone wolf is as lonely as it is artificial.

The reverse of this card warns against the thought that change will solve all problems. Stand and face your challenges, and that will initiate the positive change you need.

Panther

PROPHECY

Panther is one of the most beautiful creations of life. He is among the most powerful creatures in life; physically, mentally and spiritually. Panther is also a study in what may seem contradictory but is, in reality, perfect balance; sometimes to the immense irritations of his friends and enemies. Panther is very fierce, a warrior of tremendous strength and skill. A force to be reckoned with, others cross him at their peril. In the business of life, Panther rarely loses. He can also be very tender and gentle. In the warmth of the den, he is a loving mate and parent. In the arena of recreation, he is playful and a joy to have on your team;

while the other team wishes he was on their side.

Panther seems subject to a curious and wholly capricious eccentricity of potency. He alternates between periods of great effort and no effort. This pattern is an expression of his nature. His power comes in great bursts of energy. He accomplishes amazing feats that would seem to ask more than even his brawn could withstand, and beyond even his magnificent mind. Once the task is accomplished, Panther withdraws to recoup his vigor. It is the way of the panther to balance periods of high activity and deep rest. There is no pacing of the periods of waxing and waning energy. It is spent in heroic proportions, and recouped in languorous relaxation.

As impressive as Panther may be physically and mentally, his spiritual gifts may be the greatest of his talents. Tecumseh, a wise man, a statesman, and a visionary, was considered one of the greatest Native American leaders. He was also called "Fire in the Sky", so named because at the moment of his birth, a comet streaked across the heavens. Native Americans believed that the comet was the sign of the panther and it conferred the gift of prophecy.

Panther speaks to us about the future, about things to come. You must always remember that what is done today will affect what happens tomorrow, just as a cast stone causes outward-spreading ripples in the water. Whether it is a psychic talent or a highly analytical mind capable of processing tremendous amounts of information and producing a cogent conclusion, Panther knows what will happen.

Know, too, the balance of the universe is held in the heart of the Panther. The Great Cat speaks to us of the balance of nature, the balance of work and play, the balance of responsibility and freedom, the balance of light and dark.

Do not overlook the need for comfort and enjoyment. The great feline tells us neither strength nor intelligence is weakened by enjoying life. Yet, beware living only for the moment, for time is fleeting and the seasons change. The future, Panther tells us, is what will be, and what is now is to be savored.

When Panther chooses to reveal himself, it is to caution you to not overlook the whispering coming from the secret place in your heart, giving you advice. That is your intuition. Panther has come to assure you it is a gift and a talent to be used, not rejected. There is no need to fear it or feel guilty about having been gifted with the talent.

The reverse of this card speaks of someone who does not face the future as an opportunity, but as something dreadful. Panther encourages you to listen to your heart. Balance is not always what other people call moderation. Life can be immoderate. There are times when you are the Panther in the Sky, ablaze with glory and power. Rejoice. There are other times when you are the cat in the den enjoying the quiet warmth. Sleep.

Coyote

DECEPTION, THINGS NOT AS THEY SEEM

Though charming and at ease in social situations, Coyote enjoys his own company and becomes resentful if he is not afforded time to himself. His most important social contact is his mate. While he enjoys his children and he is as playful as a child, to the delight of all youngsters, he must have time away for peace of mind. His devotion can be destroyed, if those he loves do not understand his desperate need and read it as rejection.

When it comes to making his way in life and providing for the few souls he embraces completely, Coyote shines. He brings zest and new perspective, a willingness to learn. He can also bring about chaos. He may be the only one to survive, though he may suffer along with everyone else. He is not one of evil intentions, his exuberance is often the cause of negative results because he will sometimes act without considering the future. Coyote is often the very image of impulsiveness.

His compulsive nature aside, Coyote remains a complex, cunning creature. Coyote is a survivor with excellent instincts and the all important ability to learn lessons quickly, if only he will pay attention.

He likes to learn, though his interests in education are quixotic; sometimes based on seeking relief from boredom and sometimes seeking an increase in his fortunes. Either reason is valid, and both are laudable. It is also a positive way to keep a lively mind and exuberant spirit occupied.

Coyote has momentous talents but is often indiscriminate as to how he employs those talents. He has the capacity to be creative and constructive, but there are times when his creations are not for the purposes of good, and he can be very destructive. He can scatter stars across the heavens or spread mischief along the path.

Coyote warns us things are not always as they seem. Simple answers and snap decisions are not what is needed here. He wants you to know that deep thought and careful calculation are the way to your solutions.
Remember, deception is not always purposeful. Do not make your decisions based on superficial observations. Sometimes you are Coyote, sometimes you are dealing with Coyote. Learn to recognize the difference.

Coyote is a brilliant orator, and his story telling abilities are so good that he sometimes convinces himself his tall tales are the truth. Look deeply into the situation, consider what you are not telling yourself. Listen carefully to what others say, and you will hear the ring of truth in the conversation.

The reverse of this card tells of someone who believes deception, particularly their own. Make changes based on what you observe, for Coyote gives the gift of keen observation to those willing to accept his offering.

Golden Eagle

GOALS & AMBITION

One of the most universal symbols of mankind is the magnificent Golden Eagle. Regal, proud, and courageous, Golden Eagle is not only the sign of goals to be realized, but the ambition needed to achieve them.

Eagle was created for his beauty, to inspire hope and confidence. His presence means success and victory. He embodies the blessings of the Universe to creation.

Certainly, Eagle was blessed by the Universe with intelligence and tolerance. Though he and his mate carve out great territories, they are most gracious when it comes to permitting others to share their home, particularly the young.

Golden Eagle and his mate will act as mentors and teachers; they know there is nothing to fear from competition.

Golden Eagle will cooperate when it comes to using resources, and he uses the resources available. He is ingenious when coming up with new ideas and strategies. He will accomplish anything he sets himself upon doing. Once he's established his goal, there is nothing that can stop him. His ambition is honest and ethical, leading him to work hard and smart.

Golden Eagle is a loyal and loving mate, male or female. A partner is lifelong for Golden Eagle. A good parent, the young are protected from any harm, and even supervised during play. Golden Eagle provides the children with plenty of stimulating toys that are entertaining and educational.

Golden Eagle is a very spiritual creature; in part because of the designs of the Universe, in part because of his own nature. He is not impressed by pomp and circumstance, despite the extensive use of his image and himself in many lavish, elaborate, and very expensive ceremonies. He is impressed by that which is simple and true; the source of his elegance and his spirit.

All Eagles are sacred. It is upon their great wings that all wishes are taken to the Great Spirit, and they bring us our dreams from His dwelling place. Golden Eagle is the most powerful of the Medicine symbols, and he may be the inspiration for the form of the Thunderbird, a most sacred entity. It is said that thunderstorms are created by wind caused by their powerful wings, and that lightning shoots from their eyes.

Golden Eagle will smile if you ask him to, and he will say true success is never taking your eyes from your goals or allowing attention to be drawn from the objective. That truism is more powerful than even the Thunderbird's lightning.

Remember, Golden Eagle counsels, each day brings

you changes and new challenges. Do not be distracted from your goals. Honorable ambition is the fuel of success, it elevates and never negates. Be magnanimous in sharing your knowledge and your skills. The generous teacher learns more than even the most eager student.

The reverse of this card is a warning not to be deterred from honorable goals achieved by honorable means. It tells that turning away from the spiritual is a terrible, self-defeating loss. It also tells of the ability to change the darkness into light, to set wings to your soul and fly free.

Red Tailed Hawk

REVELATION ABOUT HOME OR FAMILY

Red Tailed Hawk is the largest of all hawks and is easily identified by his magnificent wing span as well as the rich russet color of his tail feathers. He does not migrate in the true sense of the term, though he and his mate will adjust their range to the seasons. Rather, he prefers to provide a stable environment, a good home, for his young. He is not a soul involved in many parts of the community, but wherever he dwells, he works to the benefit of his family and his neighbors. He is welcomed in any community and admired for his sense of home.

Red Tailed Hawk is the sign of things relating to home and family. A fierce protector of nest and young, Red Tail will savagely attack any intruder, even humans. Red Tail is a swift and true provider, meeting the needs of its mate and its young before its own. A good parent, both males and females sit on the eggs and care for the hatchlings. The nest is refurbished every couple of years to ensure a good and safe haven.

When Red Tailed Hawk appears, be aware of knowledge to come about your home or your family. Be aware of those around you, and be ready to put the needs of your loved ones before your own. This is not a sacrifice, it is an honor and a privilege. You will know the difference, as does Red Tail Hawk, between those in need and those who will exploit others for their own gain.

Red Tail can also signal a change in the home environment, perhaps the need to do some refurbishing of your own "nest". Make sure that you have the materials at hand to make the repairs. Remember the home is a nest, a haven for your family. It is not to be a warehouse of possessions, arranged as if in a museum, each thing to be admired but never touched. Red Tail cares for the household goods so his family may enjoy them, but he does not worship them.

The reverse of this card indicates an unwillingness to accept the revelations about home and or family. You must remember that those you love and for whom you care are, like you, individuals with hopes and dreams. Those dreams are not necessarily the ones you might wish for them. Be accepting of honorable and ethical differences, but not of selfish whims that harm others.

Red Tail can also be a warning to you about ignorance of what is happening within the family. Are you paying attention? Be certain you are not seeing what you wish to observe and overlooking what is really happening. Take steps to learn what you should already know so the Red Tail's message does not have to be "pay attention."

Jaguar

CONTROL, SELF-DETERMINATION, FREEDOM OF WILL

No feline is subject to any will but its own and the magnificent Jaguar underscores that sentiment. Control and self-determination are the hallmarks of this spirit as well as the sacred freedom of will. Jaguar counsels you to extend to others the courtesy that you demand, to expect nothing but the best, and to give no less.

Wise as well as beautiful and aloof, Jaguar seeks only the counsel of those who have proven themselves expert and worthy. He succeeds when others fail because he will not allow himself to be dissuaded. He is no fool, however, he calculates the value of the goal and, should it prove less than cost effective, he will move on to more suitable objectives.

Jaguar's spiritual life is on the highest planes of existence. He walks with angels, but even they cannot counsel him if they are unproven. He has been touched by the gods and he possesses a remarkable ability to create, destroy and recreate. Jaguar is a precious ally and a dangerous enemy. When Jaguar deigns to appear, you have been given the gift of self-realization. You must take control, you must depend on your free will and not the will of the less visionary. You have the gift of self-determination if only you will accept that you have always had the gift within yourself. Jaguar's gift is helping you unlock the chains with which you have bound your freedom.

There are times when you walk the path alone, but you are not lonely; other times you work with others. Know always that it is your will and your self-determination. You control your own destiny, and that is enough.

The reverse of Jaguar's card speaks of determination that is out of control and used as a weapon against others. It tells of free will damaged and self-determination blocked. If you are the subject of such cruelty, then show your claws. If you are the perpetrator, meditate on the phenomenon of how the enslaver often becomes enslaved.

Barn Owl

NECESSARY KNOWLEDGE

Owls have always occupied a special place in the hearts of men. The symbol of wisdom as well as loyalty, their likeness is found on the most ancient artifacts of every culture. Owls are revered not only as signs of the learned, but the learning itself.

The Owl is also a sign of great change. In some cultures, the Owl escorts the soul to the next place. Death is not what the Owl signifies, but a new and greater existence.

Barn Owl, a beautiful and highly adaptable bird, has earned a special place because it lives so closely to humans without being touched by them. It remains true to itself and its nature.

Barn Owl is unique among its fellows; distinctive not only because of his physical characteristics, but because of his voice, a rasping cry rather than the "hoot" of most large Owls. He is a good parent; both males and females work assiduously to satisfy the ravenous appetites of their young. It is his pleasure to meet the needs of his family. He delights in teaching his offspring, giving them the necessary knowledge to not only survive, but achieve. He is a problem solver and a teacher.

Barn Owl is quiet, even silent, going about his business without fanfare. His quiet nature belies good humor and strong resolution. He does not take anything at face value, he does his research. It is not enough to have a survey, he wants exact information before he makes up his mind about his next move. While decisive, he is not impulsive. Barn Owl does not confuse spontaneity with recklessness.

Barn Owl's appearance is the sign of the teacher. A good teacher knows his task is to guide the student, to help the student learn how to learn, and how to think critically.

This card tells that you must gain knowledge about your situation; learn about your problem and then you will find your solution. The problem itself holds the key to its answer. Further, you must learn not to be at the mercy of others when it comes to defining yourself. Learning from others is not the same as letting yourself be controlled by them. You are not at the mercy of fate when you are armed with necessary knowledge.

The reverse of this card tells of someone frustrated in their search for necessary knowledge. Try another path to that knowledge, do not let habit or convention limit your journey. Look to the Barn Owl for the guidance you need, to be inspired to learn, to think without allowing your emotions to run rampant. No waffling with fear, or letting your imagination run wild. Instead, harness your imagination and creativity as wonderful, winged creatures; Owls if you will, flying toward the solutions you need. Reason gives wing to thought, and the Barn Owl is the knowledge you need.

Wood Duck

PATIENCE, HARMONY WITH ENVIRONMENT

Regal and calm, the wood duck is the symbol of patience and harmony with its surroundings. Serenely swimming in waters not always calm, the Wood Ducks retains its dignity as it works to make progress without causing damage.

The male Wood Duck is a warrior, its regalia of beautiful feathers blending in with the environment or bursting out at intruders to defend the family hunting grounds. The female, more subtle but still lovely in her softer dappled color, lays her eggs in the cavities of trees and cares for the young while her mate provides food.

When it is time for the little ones to learn the lessons of

life, their parents escort them to the pond, their classroom. Wood Duck patiently teaches his young how to live in harmony with others and with their surroundings. His efforts will ensure their comfortable survival and the comfortable survival of their young.

Wood Duck moves in small, close circles, not large communities. He is skilled at finding what he and his family need to live prosperously, and he seldom strays far from his ancestral home. He adapts to his environment rather than trying to change it, but he will modify his territory to suit the family needs. Wood Duck is a master of recycling when it comes to living space, he will find an old home and turn it into a fine nest. He is a master of negotiating obstacles with ease; his spirit is such that he will not waste his energies or resources on hopeless battles with large trees.

This symbol indicates the need for cultivating patience, and working with your environment, not against it. It tells you of the need for knowing when to be in the background, and when to burst forth, ready to do battle. Wood Duck is a sensible creature; not shy, but not interested in glory. He accepts change as inevitable, and adapts to it as needed.

In reverse, Wood Duck tells you of the need to accept what you cannot change. Lessons must be learned, and experience is the only teacher. Endure and take pride in your endurance.

Leave the hopeless battles to the Don Quixotes of the world. To Wood Duck, tilting windmills is the same as trying to fly through a tree. It isn't even worth the effort to try. Use your energies wisely and if you find yourself facing a losing battle that must be fought, take the long view and not the short. It is better to gather the chestnuts that drop from the tree, than to cut down the tree. That way, your family gets a good meal, and you have effectively limited the number of trees that will grow.

Big Horn Sheep

STABILITY, INFLEXIBILITY

Big Horn Sheep is the handsome expression of stability and community. He dens in one place for many years, and forms deep attachments with both family and friends. He is not comfortable around strangers, and it takes a long time before he will welcome them, if ever. He is suspicious of anyone not already a part of the family or the community in which he was born.

Magnificent, adaptable, and very stubborn, Big Horn Sheep is a master of husbanding resources. He is not parsimonious; he is thrifty and he can live comfortably on very little. That is not to say he does not enjoy luxury, for he has an eye for quality. He is adaptable and creative within the confines of his own comfort zone.

Long recognized by People of the American West as among the toughest of animals, the Big Horn Sheep stands for both stability and inflexibility. There is virtue in stability, unless it becomes stagnation; inflexibility is not negative when it is applied to that which is ethical.

Inflexibility, when it comes to survival, is not negative. When it impairs life, learning, and love, inflexibility is tragic. It stunts growth, and waters down dreams until the dreamer becomes stunted.

The reverse of this card is indicative of someone who acts contrary to his own survival and the survival of his community. Reconsider whether you are being stable or inflexible, standing your ground or becoming stunted.

Remember that Big Horn has two sides, one a loyal lover and friend, the other a difficult, demanding autocrat. Big Horn will do battle with others just for the sake of battle. He will take his stand and stubbornly refuse to consider any other viewpoint. He will butt heads over issues that are not worth arguing over, until he and at least half the family have headaches.

Do not confuse using determination as an admirable skill with using that same determination as a weapon to badger others into submission. Willfulness is neither fact nor logic. Trying to force others to concede your point of view will only gain lip service, not agreement. Life is too short to force people into lying to you.

Gray Squirrel

PREPARATION, AWARENESS

Few creatures are as admired for the ability to prepare in advance for hard times as Gray Squirrel. Nature has endowed Squirrel with the ability to select and cache food during the times when resources are scarce. Human legends frequently point to Gray Squirrel as an example of maintaining an awareness of possibilities as well as preparing for those possibilities.

Gray Squirrel's preparations go far beyond dealing with potential disaster. He prepares for other eventualities as well, including the probability of needing more room for his family. He will build a nest with a spacious nursery and several nests very near the main home.

Gray Squirrel is ever aware of his surroundings, and he teaches his children to be equally as alert. He counsels against confrontation, unless the stakes are very high. Rather, he remains in the background, working on his home, enjoying his family and living a comfortable life.

When Gray Squirrel comes to you, it is to tell you there is a need to make preparations or to increase them. There is also a need to be more aware of your surroundings, the people around you, and the events just beginning to unfold.

Your preparations must be considered not only for the bad times, but the good. What are the ramifications of your actions? Are you prepared to accept success, or will you find yourself mourning the lack of struggle that has proven so invigorating over the years? Awareness of your environment and the beings who inhabit it with you does not mean you are necessarily under attack. It may be that you are overlooking special friendship, even romance because you aren't paying attention.

In reverse, the Gray Squirrel tells us of a situation that is not foreseen and for which you cannot be fully prepared. Be aware that some situations are a surprise, and you must, like Gray Squirrel, be prepared to face the unexpected.

Bobcat

SELF-SUFFICIENCY, SECRECY, HOLDING
ONE'S OWN COUNSEL

Bobcat is the epitome of individualism. He goes about his own business, and takes care of what needs doing. He will tackle projects and problems that are not only larger than he is, but larger than life itself, and succeed with aplomb. Bobcat is the very image of the self-sufficient, decisive soul.

However, such a solo individual is not a builder of communities and fellowship. He does not need others to stimulate his intellectual curiosity, to keep him company, or to help him in his given career. He tends to prefer working in an area where he is in control and usually working alone.

His family life often appears to be dysfunctional, but in reality, it works very nicely as long as his mate's personality matches his. Bobcat children are keepers of secrets, highly ethical, and good problem solvers. As a child or an adult, Bobcat can be obsessive about any subject that interests him, and stubbornly disinterested concerning anything else. He often becomes expert in his own field of endeavor, and is unperturbed by his ignorance of other areas.

Bobcat as a mother is a fierce protector of her children, even refusing to let their father help until they are older. Bobcat fathers provide what their young need, and help teach them to be independent. Bobcats often have trouble with close relationships since their solitary nature results in a behavior that is often misunderstood as rejection.

Bobcat wants his time alone, and the subject is not open to discussion, not even with his mate. His love can be earned by someone as self-sufficient as he, but it can be lost if there is too much talk about "getting in touch with feelings and then sharing them." Bobcat is in touch with his feelings and if he wants to share them, he will do so without anyone's prompting. Mostly, he wants his privacy and to walk his path undisturbed by annoying chatter.

Tell a secret to Bobcat, and he will carry it to his grave. Ask his advice, and he will tell you to figure out your own problems because you have to live with the consequences. He will, however, direct you to the information you need to solve the problem.

Bobcat tells of a time to be self-sufficient. Secrecy and holding one's own counsel are advisable at this juncture; do not betray confidences. Others are not entitled to everything you know, think, or feel. Learn to hold your tongue, observe and learn. Remember, too, self-sufficiency is not the same thing as selfishness; do not confuse the two. You must learn to rely on yourself, not lean on others, for they have their own lives to attend.

You must become expert in your own affairs, your own business. A lively interest in everything, but a lack of expertise in anything is the life of an underachiever. Bobcat reminds you that you must survive, and that you cannot depend on others for your survival. You have talents, develop them. Choose what interests you, not someone else. Worry less about what others do and what they say. Do not trouble yourself over the opinions of others unless they have something useful to say. Do what you do, do it well and do it with pride. Bobcat tells you the only real accomplishment in life is what you do yourself. There is nothing wrong or sinful about honest pride.

The reverse of this card tells of someone in your life who cannot keep a secret. It can also warn of a time when you need to work with others rather than alone, when keeping a secret harms the one you are trying to protect. You will need to face that sometimes you must deal with others, taking into account their needs and desires, even thought you would sooner walk away, disappearing into the quiet woods where you have your precious solitude.

Follow your own counsel, as does the Bobcat; but listen to your counsel, not your wishful thinking.

Sparrow Hawk

FARSEEING, ABLE TO SEE THE ENTIRE PICTURE

High above the land, Sparrow Hawk glides on air currents, and looks at the land below. He sees what our ancestors could only imagine, the lakes and rivers, the valleys and mountains. For him, life is a patchwork of color and patterns, opportunities that may be overlooked by those too close to the ground present themselves to him constantly.

Sparrow Hawk is highly adaptable, able to make his home and do his work anywhere. He enjoys his life, at work or at play. He loves his comforts, despite the amount of discomfort he may endure to get any job done.

Sparrow Hawk is extremely handsome, and it may be surprising to learn that he is far from prissy. He does not disdain dirty work, though he has no intention of making a career out of anything that will leave him hot and sweaty every day. His trim, lean form may lead you to believe he is careful about what he consumes and that he is only interested in food as a necessity, but nothing could be farther from the truth. He loves to eat. Plain, simple fare as well as magnificent, multi-course meals are greeted with enthusiasm. He is the one who always seems able to find the best little tidbit, the best item on the menu. Fortunately for his friends and family, he enjoys sharing his good taste and good fortune.

His ability to see the big picture makes being petty or secretive seem very foolish and a waste of time, energy and good will. His munificence should stand as a lesson to all.

When Sparrow Hawk comes to you, he counsels you to stop wasting your energy worrying about what you cannot control or correct. Start applying your energy toward doing what needs to be done. Sparrow Hawk points out that a high rise is just as tall as a decent hill with a sizable tree, so stop fussing. If you want to create, but you think you can't because conditions are not right, then you are making excuses Sparrow Hawk warns. If you really want to do something, decide to do it, and then follow through.

Don't let a lack of vision, or the lack of vision in others, dissuade you from trying. What is the big picture? What do you see on the horizon, and how are you going to reach it?

You must be farseeing like Sparrow Hawk. Cultivate the ability to see past the details and understand that each part is only a piece of the overall pattern. Each stroke of the brush is only a part of the picture. As Sparrow Hawk flies overhead, know that your spirit can see all of existence, if only you will permit it to do so.

In reverse, Sparrow Hawk reminds us that while each detail is only a portion of the greater picture, those details must not be neglected. Those who are farseeing understand how neglect of details can build up a negative force and spoil everything in the end.

Raccoon

EXPERIENCE, CURIOSITY, INVESTIGATION

The seeker of knowledge does well to observe Raccoon. He is a soul who learns from experience, and applies those lessons with diligence. His curiosity is satisfied only by thorough investigation. It is not an overstatement to say Raccoon is a wellspring of wisdom.

Raccoon is the innovator, adaptable and willing to use whatever resources are at hand. His curiosity compels him to experiment. He investigates. He is also a survivor who has learned not only to live with humankind, but to profit from the association without losing any part of his wild nature.

Should Raccoon decide a situation requires confrontation, he will rear on his hind legs and raise his head proudly. He is more than capable of handling any kind of situation, including those which are unpleasant. Raccoon does not charge into confrontations, nor does he perform overtly threatening displays, rather he simply reminds the agitator with whom they are dealing. This tactful reminder is usually more than enough.

A superior teacher, Raccoon counsels us to gain experience, to cherish curiosity, and investigate to gain knowledge as well as information. Are you proceeding based on what you hope or what you know? Discard the myths of truth, and find truth itself. Do not follow the herd of those who bray out an opinion without troubling themselves to discover the facts of a situation first. Avoid decisions based on the superficial. You must make decisions and changes based on solid, well-researched facts, and intelligent, informed opinions from those who, like Raccoon, do their homework before they open their mouths, put their money on the line, or ruin someone else's life.

Raccoon reminds us to stand our ground in a calm, polite, but very firm manner. You must stand your ground, particularly, when faced with that herd whose population has already made up its collective mind and really does not want to be faced with the facts of a situation. It is nothing to fight over, Raccoon tells us. A forthright reminder is the answer to most conflicts, not outright war. They'll sulk a little, but they'll get over it and move on, just as you will.

In reverse, the raccoon tells us to use our experience to know when we need new knowledge and when we need to stop gathering information and get to work. Investigation has a point, and that point is to accomplish our goals. When the investigation becomes the point, we have forgotten our purpose.

Raccoon also tells us that sometimes standing our ground does come at a cost, and sometimes we really do have endure unpleasantness in order to ensure that justice prevails. Raccoon, however, is equal to such tasks and he reminds us that so are we.

Ocelot

PROCRASTINATION, AVOIDANCE, RELUCTANCE

In Ocelot, man finds one of the most beautiful creations of the Universe, not only in face and body, but also intelligence and spirit. He is adaptable and cunning, using all of his talents to make his way through life. Ocelot uses all of his skills (physical, mental and psychic) to live life his own way. Ocelot learns from experience, and he is reserved and wary. He will tell you, if you will only listen, that those who may seem trustworthy often are not. Further, he cautions, those who think themselves moral and preach morality are often the least ethical. Ocelot knows each of them for who they are, and he avoids them. Further, he teaches his young to live quietly, but well away from prying eyes and those who would exploit them.

However, Ocelot is not a hermit eschewing all companionship. A soul loyal and true, Ocelot loves not easily, but deeply. Once he has made a friend, he cherishes the friendship. However, Ocelot is reluctant to move quickly toward anything, including relationships. He tends to avoid any form of confrontation. He practices procrastination as a high art form.

Ocelot warns us that sometimes we must go slowly. Survival is as much instinct and psychic hunches as it is information. If you are reluctant to plunge into a new adventure or to confront an old problem, ask yourself "why?" Ocelot takes his time rather than taking the risk of being someone's trophy.

Ocelot counsels us to listen to our instincts, to understand the basis of evasion. From him, we learn the difference between the distasteful and the dangerous.

There are times when procrastination may have some redeeming value. Precisely whose priority is the task at hand, anyway? Stand before yourself as judge, and ask yourself whether or not you are procrastinating because you are reluctant and fearful, or because you have other pressing concerns of your own. If you are reluctant and fearful, then Ocelot has come to tell you to plunge out of the brush, and run along the path. If you have other concerns, then Ocelot has appeared to tell you to slip quietly into the woods, and to stop letting others run your life.

In reverse, the Ocelot councils us to throw off our reluctance, our procrastination, our avoidance. We should face our fears, but not get shot for false bravado. This time, procrastination, avoidance, and reluctance are not at all redeeming; they are obstacles, not tools.

Do not listen to those who would preach themselves as better than you. For no one who holds himself above others is worth the price of the air he uses. See the souls, not the bodies; hear the meaning of the words, and not the sweet sounds. Be as discriminating as the Ocelot, and strive to be as beautiful in your heart as he has been created.

Dall's Sheep

CONFIDENCE, SUPPORT

Dall's Sheep survives where others have failed because of supreme confidence in his ability to live in an environment that can, at best, be called harsh. Seemingly inaccessible heights, cavernous deeps, and jagged rocks do not deter Dall's Sheep. He relies not only on his self-confidence, but on the support of his family and community. The Dall's Sheep is both an individual and one of many. He can rely on the herd, and the herd can rely on him.

When Dall's Sheep comes to you, he is telling you that your lack of confidence may be because you think you should never call on others for support. There is a difference between being dependent and receiving support from friends and family. Do not confuse a genuine offer of help as a sign of pity. Do not confuse accepting help with being weak. You are being treated as an equal, and you must be ready to offer support to others whenever possible. That is not a society of the weak, but a community standing shoulder-to-shoulder against all odds.

You must face whatever it is that drains your confidence. You must determine whether something frightens you because it is a change and you feel uncomfortable about, or if it is because you do not have the skills to solve the problem. If you are uncomfortable, why? You can't expect yourself to be excellent in everything. There are very few people who are good at everything, though many may claim to be. Or, is this something that troubles your ethics? Does it trouble your well being or that of your loved ones, or the community? Once you know, make your decision.

If it is unethical or dangerous, leap away like Dall's Sheep bounding up the rocky hillside. If it is uncomfortable because you do not have the skills to handle the situation, then learn those skills. If you find that even your new skills aren't quite enough, then turn to someone who has the abilities to help you solve the problem. Chances are, you have talents that person would be glad to have applied to problems they have to solve. Remember: Community, Confidence and Support. Dall's Sheep says those must be your watch words from now on. When change comes, face it armed with those precious words and the great concepts behind them.

The concepts that will help you are to gain any and all skills needed to develop confidence. Know that you can rely on yourself. Learn to rely on the support of others as well as to support others. Know when the job requires the efforts of the individual, and when it requires the united efforts of the herd.

The reverse of the Dall's Sheep card indicates a lack of confidence. If you are not getting the support you need, why not? Are you pursuing a goal that is against the values of your family or community? Is that goal worthy of you? If so, then seek the support and confidence of those who do not consider you property or a servant, but an individual who is part of the community. If not, then re-evaluate your reasons for trying to attain a goal that has turned your fellows against you.

Woodchuck

ANALYSIS, ATTENTION TO DETAIL

Woodchuck is also known as Groundhog, and he is a complex soul. When you look at the homey Woodchuck, you see a solid citizen who loves his mate and adores his children. Obviously, he enjoys a good dinner, and he is sociable enough (but not a party animal). He really doesn't have much going for him. He seems content to go about his business, pleasant in form and manner, but what could be spectacular about this soul? Learn now, appearances really can be deceiving.

Woodchuck is a being of great and useful talents. He provides for his family and he takes his responsibilities seriously. He has a sense of humor and an even better sense of creativity. For an example, one may look at his home. It is testimony to an immense bastion of talent.

Woodchuck dwells below ground in a series of tunnels of his own making; a complex feat of engineering. In order to accomplish this feat of construction, it is necessary to analyze the lay of the land, the soil, and take into consideration rainfall as well as predators. Attention to detail is the key.

When Woodchuck comes to you, he has come to tell you to use your good sense to analyze what is happening and what is going to happen. Do not build your dreams in shifting soil where they might be smothered, or in places where they may be rent apart by the chatter of others. There are times when you must endure, but many more times when you must understand you have the control. However, you can lose control if you do not pay attention to what may seem right now to be petty details. This time, you cannot make your way by understanding only the larger picture. You must comprehend every level.

Further, Woodchuck counsels, you must use your new found, or reawakened, ability to analyze, to judge what you must do. Again, it is the attention to detail that will ensure that you ride out the coming change. You will, with care, emerge unscathed rather than suffering. There is no part of your life that you can overlook at this juncture. Your life must be the psychic version of Woodchuck's tunnels.

As you make your way through the great change that is about to take hold, remember Woodchuck's counsel. Woodchuck warns you not to advance unless you have an idea of a plan. If you come to an unexpected obstacle, dig over it, around it or under it, but do not let it stop you. Pay attention to the details, and the master plan will take form like Woodchuck's tunnels beneath the earth.

The reverse of this card is not only a warning to stop and analyze your situation, it is also a warning that there is a time when analysis stops and the work begins. Over-attention to detail, as a means of delay or avoidance, is as bad as no attention at all. A bad construction with great details is still in danger of collapse.

Bald Eagle

COURAGE

Bald Eagle is an adaptable soul. He learns from experience, and he is willing to try new approaches to problem solving. He is ready to take advantage of any opportunity that comes his way, and if necessary, he will go looking for opportunity. He has the courage of his resolve, and he ignores his fears. It is better, he will tell you, to go forth and fly like an Eagle, than sit safe and surrounded by your fears, wondering what flying might be like.

    Brave soul that he is, there are still times when it seems as if Bald Eagle is as inert as a bronze image of himself. Do not be fooled. He misses nothing, and he will take to wing with barely the breath of notice.

Bald Eagle, so observant and opportunistic a creature, is a good provider. He is also a loyal mate and loving parent. Once he has chosen his mate, it is forever, and once he has decided on a place to live, he stays. You will find Bald Eagle in a handsome nest with an awe inspiring view, putting down roots that will give rise to genealogical trees of mammoth proportions.

Bald Eagle is courage, conviction and personal belief. Like the Golden Eagle, the "white-headed Eagle" is a powerful sign, regal and independent. He tells us to be proud, not prideful; and to take pride in what we do, not what has been done.

Bald Eagles teaches that we will better survive by being adaptable; using what is at hand. Do not despair at what is not within your grasp, but use what is available. Bald Eagle winks and tells you to accept less in order to gain more.

Do not, Bald Eagle counsels, waver from your beliefs or your convictions regardless of what life presents. Only walk away if you discover your beliefs and convictions have been based on falsehoods or misleading information. Do your research, use your "Eagle's Eye" to discern fact from fiction, and then have the courage to fly like a soul taking to wing.

Eagle is the symbol of the Sky God, the Thunderbird. He possesses extraordinary vision and soars to extraordinary heights. With conviction and belief, all things are possible. The greatest medicine is represented by and bestowed by Eagle.

When Bald Eagle comes, he tells of a spirit that must soar, learn, and communicate. Our prayers and wishes are taken to the Great Spirit on the wings of Eagles, and answers are brought back to us, floating on the celestial wind like feathers drifting in the air. Bald Eagle tells you, "Do not chain that spirit. Set it free."

The reverse of Bald Eagle's card speaks of a spirit trapped, of a mind that has been closed. Let your mind and soul follow the Thunderbird to the limits of the sky, and accept the invitation to be greeted by the Great Spirit.

Gray Fox

DISAPPOINTMENT

Charming and attractive, the Gray Fox is also cunning and wise. Foxes are curious by nature; they investigate everything. Gray Fox is a problem solver; a scholar and a detective who relies on his wits not only to protect himself, but to save others. He is a good teacher who opens the minds of his young to the possibilities, gives them the tools they need to find what they need, and lets them learn.

He is an inventive soul, given to somewhat unorthodox methods of solutions, and we would do well to follow his lead. Many times Gray Fox has outwitted his enemies by executing brilliant, unexpected strategies. While his pursuers scratch their heads in bewilderment, disappointed and frustrated, Gray Fox rests comfortably in the tree tops, enjoying the view and having the good grace to not laugh too loudly. You didn't know Gray Fox could climb trees? You can, too!

Though Gray Fox may signify disappointment, now you know why he is not to be avoided. He has wise counsel for you, and seeks to help you avoid the gloomy portent. The sign of the Gray Fox tells of disappointment born not of outside circumstances but of those inside yourself. It is not a matter of lowering one's expectations, it is a matter of following the road and finding out what is at the end without expecting anything but the answer.

You have little to fear from your enemies. Many are not really enemies, but so interested in their own advancement they barely notice you. You merely need to climb that lovely tree and stay out of the way. You are not quitting, you are simply elevating yourself to a higher plane, a greater vision, freeing yourself of the dusty trail everyone else is trying to follow. You, Gray Fox urges, must be where the air is clean, the sun warm, the shade cool, and opportunities present themselves as ripe fruit nearly bursting and ready to take.

The reverse of the Gray Fox card marks coming disappointment born of a failure to investigate. True, the fruits of the investigation may prove bitter, but do the research, even if you fear the answer. Failure to act like the Gray Fox may end with you in the trap.

Red Fox

REGRET, RECRIMINATION

Red Fox is a charmer; he seems to play, but he's hard at work. He doesn't appear to be paying attention, but he misses nothing. Let the window of cosmic opportunity open, even a tiny crack, and watch Red Fox dive through.

Intelligent and independent, Red Fox often prefers to walk his path alone, but he is a good provider and an excellent parent. Red Fox as a mother is devoted to her young. She cares for them and teaches. Red Fox as a father is tireless in keeping his family steeped in comfort. He takes his share of parental duties, teaching and playing with his kits. Both parents continue to take an interest in their children's lives even after the first steps to their own independence. Like good parents everywhere, they make sure their young adults have enough to eat and stay clear of traps. Red Fox as a young adult does pay attention to his parents, and he is happy to accept supper now and again.

So enchanting a personality, it is no wonder Red Fox is the charmer of many tales; sometimes teaching, sometimes learning lessons. Often, these lessons are hard. Do not despair when you see the beautiful Red Fox peeking at you with a wink. He has a smile, and he is here to teach you how to change for the better.

Red Fox tells us we have a right to our regrets and even our recriminations, but he warns us to indulge in our own emotional stew for a very short time. Red Fox advises we must learn to put both aside in order to change our path.

The arrival of Red Fox is a hopeful sign. Red Fox is a powerful magician, he can change himself as well as his path. The lesson Red Fox teaches us is that we can change ourselves in order to walk a better road. No one can do that for us, and we can do it for no one else. It is true magic.

Red Fox also reminds us that one who has advanced at the expense of others must repent and give redress. The recriminations of Red Fox can be very unforgiving, he is the person of our good conscience and our ethics.

Lastly, Red Fox reminds us to play for the sheer joy of playing. Be silly, be childlike, do things just to do them. Your heart will soar and that window of opportunity in the cosmos will turn out to be hands reaching to share their joy as you share yours.

The reverse of the Red Fox card speaks of one who must reconsider goals and ask why they are causing problems. Are you facing jealousy because of your ambition? Then proceed, but with kindness and nobility. Have you begun to achieve your goals at the cost of depriving others? Then stop, or face the consequences.

The reverse of Red Fox's card is also a warning to heed our inner voices when our souls warn us of the potential for regret and for recrimination. Do not turn away when Red Fox speaks, even though you may not want to hear what he has to say. Are you making a decision too fast? Based on fear and not investigation? Are you setting yourself up for later regrets? Do not open yourself to the recriminations of others, any more than you would let loose your own recriminations as though they were arrows of anger.

Kit Fox

CONCERN, FEAR

Though sometimes overlooked and misunderstood, Kit Fox, a tiny gem of creation, has an important place in the pantheon of the spirits. See him not as a timid creature, but a creature with valuable experience who whispers rather than shouts. Know him for the charming, clever soul he is, and for the kind spirit he possesses.

He is a caring soul who will give you the benefit of his experience and knowledge. But you must listen very carefully, for he will not force the issue. Kit Fox is a teacher to whom you must be attentive. He says as much by means of sign and symbol as he does in words, perhaps more.

Remember, he tells you, there is often more to be learned by observation than by speech. Know the truth when you see it; sometimes it will be in a raised eyebrow, the way a man stands, or how a woman holds her hands.

Kit Fox knows how suddenly life can change, and he has become wary of too much change too fast. He comes to tell you not to let yourself be overwhelmed. You must treat each event in your life both individually and as part of the greater whole. Everything is interconnected, but nothing can be dealt with as a huge bundle. Separate facts from fiction, dreams from myths, hopes from fears.

Kit Fox warns of reasons to be concerned and not to dismiss feelings of fear. Kit Fox is the symbol of trusting your instincts. Kit Fox tells you to heed that silent communication of movement and expression. Your instincts will tell you if you have something about which to be concerned or to fear. Do not dismiss your ability to read the silent language of motion.

The Kit Fox tells you to be ever alert to your environment as well as to those sharing it with you, however near or far they are to you. There is no shame in retreating from situations you cannot win. Wisdom is knowing the difference between idle interest and real concern. Concern and fear are the Great Spirit's warning signals, Kit Fox counsels. Pay attention.

There is a time to be filled with bravado, and a time to be quiet in the shadows. Reflect upon the appropriateness of the situation. Are you standing ground you have no right to stand? Are you fighting a fight you have no hope of winning? Or perhaps you have no right to win?

The reverse of the card is admonishment. He warns of a mind dismissing the communications from the soul. The body is a temporary thing, the soul is eternal. Heed its warnings, and do not be dissuaded from the path of the Kit Fox, one of nature's beloved survivors.

Arctic Fox

CONTRADICTION, CONFLICT

Arctic Fox is the only member of the Fox family whose appearance changes from season to season. During the harsh, cruel winters of the arctic, his coat is pristine white. During the difficult summers, the snowy hued coat is shed, and one of earth tone shades is revealed. When caught between summer and winter, Arctic Fox must be wary and employ all of his cunning ways not only to capture prey, but to avoid becoming prey.

Arctic Fox is an enviable provider and also an admirable survivor. He lives in an environment that demands vigilance, where things seem unchanging even as they are ever changing. He must live by his wits in order to live well, and more importantly, see that his family lives as well. He faces adversity with resolve and is reluctant to accept anything at face value. Of all the lessons one may learn, and all the changes one may experience, learning the lesson Arctic Fox offers is among the most crucial. What are the facts beneath the superficial? Have you heard all sides of the story before you decide which side to take? Should you be taking sides at all? Are the words you hear being touted as fact or gossip?

Arctic Fox reminds us that humans often accept the first version of any story they are told, stubbornly resisting changes, even if they are fact. They also like their stories like the landscape of his winter home, stark white and midnight black. But there are so many shades of grey and green and blue and yellow! Be discriminating, be investigative, be alert. Change is sometimes the gathering of facts.

Arctic Fox teaches that you must be aware of contradictions, and that you must reconcile conflict in order to survive. Your future and that of your family depends upon you. Arctic Fox sees the contradiction of hunter and hunted, the conflicts that result, and those must be resolved by careful thought.

The reverse of this card warns of not taking your intuition seriously, of relying entirely on what appear to be facts, but are not necessarily true. If things don't seem quite right, then trust your instincts. Change your tunnel vision to one of broad enlightenment. See the colors around you, and notice who tends to tell you the facts and who tells you the fanciful tales. Do not build your truths on the shifting sands of fancy. Instead, dig deep into the snow, and find the green grass of truth.

Badger

GOOD LUCK, FAVORABLE EVENTS

Badger is a tenacious, brave soul who will gallantly defend the sett, his home, with every ounce of strength in his body. If you are his guest, you will find him a good and hospitable host, generous and cheerful in his own way. You will also find his home immaculately clean, handsomely designed and beautifully appointed. There will be little in the home that is not functional, and you will rarely find anything in Badger's home that is simply for show. Even the showcase items will have had some utilitarian purpose at one time, put on display not to just be admired, but to judge how much progress has been made. He is impatient with collections that just collect dust.

Badger is famous for having a temper, but that reputation is unwarranted. It is not a temper he has, but conviction and purpose. He stands his ground on principle, and the only ones who criticize his refusal to tolerate bad behavior or poor conditions are those guilty of one or responsible for the other.

Overall, Badger's strength of personality is positive, and he will do anything for a loved one or a friend. Badger is a fine parent and a skillful provider; kith and kin will never want for good food and a comfortable bed as long as he draws breath.

The appearance of Badger means good luck and favorable events. Badger also teaches us to use the talents with which we have been blessed, as well as to employ those talents in positive ways. Further, he warns us to beware of our own less than sociable behaviors, telling us that being irascible for no other reason than temper is not a good habit to keep.

Legend tells us that Badger is one of the oldest animals, created when all life was below the surface of the earth. Life in the Below World was good, but very dark. Badger decided to see what the Above World was like, and he tunneled his way to the light. Hence, Badger is not only is a leader and a seeker of knowledge, he is one who engineers the advent of favorable events. Badger tells us that just because we can live in the dark, that does not mean we must stay there.

Badger's card means you can change your luck. The events you bring about will be favorable to you and yours. Remember, however, that changes in fortune are mixed blessings, and even the happiest of fortunes will bring new circumstances that you must be ready to address.

The reverse of this card is a sign that you are failing to recognize your own role in your luck, and ignoring the possibilities. Events of good fortune unfold, but you must be aware and chose what you want–but based on realistic facts, not fantasy.

Elk

Widely admired, Elk is an active member of the community in which he lives. However, he does not rely upon anyone for his success. He relies on his own strengths and his own energies. He will give help whenever it is needed and he will accept help if needed, but he makes his own success. Elk makes his own luck through observation and gracious dignity. Elk works to understand others and is generous in granting forgiveness. He forgives those who have hurt him when they ask. In forgiveness is the grant of luck and success.

Success is action; it is using strength to rise to any occasion, not some thing to be jealously guarded or envied. Strength, Elk understands, comes not just from physical, but mental and spiritual energies. Success comes from the strength of spirit and the energy of determination to make the changes that must be made. Throw off the old wool of the winter's despair. This is the springtime of your new life, wear your new attitude as a clean, light coat. Taste the sweet new fruits that will come to you, if only you will try them.

Teacher Elk tells us to learn to see opportunities in any occasion. Proceed with dignity and kindness, do not indulge in grudges or useless retaliations against those who have slighted you during your journey to success. Discard your hurt feelings and begin anew.

The reverse of the Elk's card is a lack of energy that depletes your strength and blocks your success. Address the physical as well as the psychological and the psychic. Do not take up the worn winter coat of care after you have torn it away. Do not retreat into the mournful darkness of grudges and anger. Why mope at the back of the herd when you can run in the thick of it, or better yet, lead the way? And if you want to, why not leap into the air for the pure joy of being able to do so?

Screech Owl

COOPERATION, DOMESTIC ORGANIZATION

The tiny missionary of the gods, Screech Owl is a good mate and a fine parent. Humans have long admired Screech Owl because he is cooperative and community-minded. He much prefers discussion and peaceful solutions to quarreling or fighting. Make no mistake, however, by thinking Screech Owl's preference for peace is a sign of being docile or weak. He is an impassioned advocate, ethical and intelligent. Do not attempt to argue any point with Screech Owl without being fully prepared. You will lose because he is always prepared.

Screech Owl is a good companion, an excellent ally. He can be fierce if he must, and the same passion that fuels him as an advocate is the same energy that fires him as a warrior. He will stand and fight. Many a bully has discovered, to his dismay, the error of his ways after forcing a fight with Screech Owl.

Throughout human history, Screech Owl has been revered as a sign of home, hearth, community, and blessings. His abilities to provide for his family, his skills as a mate, parent, friend and community member, and his talent for organization are all reasons for admiration. Further evidence of how he earned his special place in the pantheon is his spiritual life.

Screech Owl communicates with the Above Ones. He tells of need and deed, he speaks of resolution and redress. Most of all, he counsels forgiveness and cooperation.

When Screech Owl comes to you, he speaks of the need for cooperation. You must not try to operate as if you are alone, for that is not domestic organization. It is an unappreciated martyrdom; you are seen as a dictator, and you feel like a victim. Family is cooperation, not domination.

Everyone needs a role to play, a contribution to make. Perhaps you can do the job better and faster, but the satisfaction of teaching another to do the job, not to mention the pride they garner learning, far outweighs the need for efficiency. Screech Owl urges the same cooperative approach in everything you do; the same domestic organization works whether it is your family or a huge corporate complex. Everyone needs to play a role in order to feel a part of the organization; not an outcast.

You must enlist the aid of others. Screech Owl also tells of the need to not only get your affairs in order, but to help the members of your family, including dear friends, organize their affairs as well. Chaos cannot rule at this time, it is time for alliances.

The reverse of the Screech Owl card is a plea to realize the need for cooperation and the necessity of domestic organization. All creatures need organization in their home life. Whatever the pressures or attractions of your outside life, stop for a while and tend to your home.

You are also warned that organization without cooperation is destructive not spiritual, and is certainly not an environment in which to teach. Screech Owl cautions you to remember each of us is here to learn, to apply what we have learned and then, to teach.

Great Horned Owl

AUTHORITY, TAKING CONTROL, OPPORTUNITY

A symbol of wisdom and authority, Great Horned Owl seizes control because he is qualified to do so, and makes the most of opportunities. No indecision here; move as Owl moves, strong, silent, and swift. Owl tells us take the moment.

Great Horned Owl is the symbol of earthly wisdom as well as spiritual enlightenment. He is not a messenger, but an emissary. He comes on a mission to represent and advance the will of all that is good.

When Great Horned Owl comes to you, it is to announce that you must start your education anew. What you learn is not only to your advantage, but an offering to the Universe; for as you enrich your life, you enrich others' lives. No material sacrifice, no weeks of fasting, nothing is as precious an offering to the Universe as enlightenment. Heaven itself rejoices when you work not only to learn, but to understand and see everything from more than one side.

Become an authority, take control, accept the opportunities you will be offered, but first understand the truth of what Horned Owl is telling you. Do not be content with superficial definitions that are easy and compact. Look deeper for the wisdom of Owl.

When he speaks of authority, Horned Owl does not mean anything so petty as control. He is speaking of real authority, knowledge. A true leader understands he is the servant, not the ruler. Strive to nurture, to educate and to learn. When Owl counsels you to take control, he is encouraging you to make the changes in your life you need to grow and to learn. No one can control anyone else without the loss of one's freedom and the other's soul.

The Owl also symbolizes life and death, for it is the Owl who takes the souls to the next world even as the Eagle carries our prayers heavenward. Know that this is not the end, Owl teaches, but the beginning. Learn.

Great Horned Owl counsels you to be unafraid of challenges. These are the opportunities not to be wasted. Spread your wings and soar to heaven. Heaven does not want your spirit to crawl.

The reverse of this card indicates someone who is ruthless. Beware of this influence, it is not the true path. Remember, success is taking what you need from life, and not wasting resources. The Great Horned Owl, sign of authority, control and opportunity, wastes nothing. Impressing others is beneath the magnificent bird's notice.

Snowy Owl

SECRETS, HIDDEN KNOWLEDGE,
UNDERSTANDING TO BE GAINED

In the silence of white winter, the Snowy Owl offers understanding. Secrets are buried under the blanket of crystal, knowledge hidden away, waiting to be discovered. Live life as though it is a loan, not a gift. Survive, learn, and return the loan better than it was lent.

Active during the day rather than night, Snowy Owl migrates from the north to the south, perching on barns, haystacks, almost anything but a tree, as it watches over its frozen domain.

Snowy Owl tells of secrets held and hidden knowledge. There is understanding to be gained by those who search. Nothing will come to you from the Owl, you must find the treasure of knowledge.

The reverse of the Snowy Owl tells of an impasse in your life. Someone important in your life has not taken the time to learn what must be known and understood. If it is you, then set about gaining the knowledge of the wise Owl. If it is a family member or friend, then encourage that person to embark upon the journey of knowledge. Teach what you know, and in the teaching you will also learn.

Osprey

INSPIRES CREATIVITY, DESIRE TO SUCCEED

Osprey is a tenacious individual who will not let success slip away. He holds on with every ounce of resolve he can muster and then he musters more. He knows there is no one way to succeed. He approaches every problem with an open mind and the idea that the solution is to be found somewhere in the problem itself. He will change his tactics should such a tactic be called for, and he makes his plans elastic rather than concrete.

As individualistic as Osprey may be, he is still reasonably social. Do not look to him for more than advice, it will not occur to him that you need, much less want, a helping hand. To him that is a low form of interference. He protects the very young, but once they have reached adolescence, he expects them to act as adults, as he did. Experience, he insists, is to be gained not given.

It is to Osprey that the seeker of creativity and the individualistic spirit should look. Osprey is the soul of solution, and therefore, the symbol of the desire for success. The desire to succeed, Osprey knows, is the key to success. For this, as well as beauty and strength, Osprey is admired in every part of the world. Conservatives and revolutionaries alike see him as the leader of success.

Drawing the Osprey card tells you to listen to the creative urges that cry out to be fulfilled like birds need to take to wing. Your desire to succeed will be realized only when you admit that the risks you fear are nothing compared to the sadness of never trying. No one can do this for you, you must do it yourself. You are walking a path walked by very few. Look to Osprey for inspiration, for a model of desire, but figure things out for yourself.

The reverse of the Osprey card tells you to work to be creative, no matter how small or large the effort. You have been waiting for success, it will not come. Go out and find it; for success hunted is success earned, and that is the satisfaction you seek.

Moose

PLANNING, GOODWILL,
ABILITY TO ASSESS A SITUATION

Moose has a special place in the legends and lore of the Universe. A soul of good will and family values, he is cheerful and cooperative. He has the ability to assess any situation, and plan for any contingency. He is a good thinker, someone who is far seeing and a soul who takes change in stride. Catastrophe is something he accepts as a possibility, not as an excuse not to plan.

Moose is a willing teacher. He shares what he knows generously and kindly. He will help you, but not do it for you. Like any good teacher, he knows much of the learning is in the doing, not the watching. Look to him for excellent advice, comfort, and good jokes.

The tribe of the Moose travels great distances, moving from one area of forage to another. The tribe lives in a large community of families, sharing their experiences and teaching the next generation what they know. They have learned where the best water and pasture lie, and they have made their plans. The family of Moose are souls of goodwill, only provoked by poor manners or aggression.

Warring with the tribe of Moose is a losing proposition and best left to those who have a high stake in the battle. Moose is more apt to reconcile than go to war, but he has his limits, and they stop at his ethics. He will not compromise his morality or the safety of his kind. He uses his keen assessment skills very quickly for defense, much to the consternation of whomever he may be confronting.

Cultivate the ability to assess a situation. Approach all situations with goodwill, not with negative preconceptions or anxiety, which can paralyze the liveliest of minds. Only wreak havoc if you are attacked and cannot survive to walk away. Choose your battles, as does the great Moose, with care.

The reverse of this card indicates a tendency to cultivate anxiety rather than gather information, a tendency to begin believing worst case scenarios as fact, rather than possibilities. Do not strike out, assess the situation first.

Canada Goose

TRAVEL, MIGRATION,
STRENGTH TO DO WHAT MUST BE DONE

The handsome Canada Goose is a member of a clan system. He uses his individual talents to work with the rest of the clan to survive and ensure the survival of the community.

Travel in the form of migration is the hallmark of the Canada Goose. Twice each year, the Geese muster enough strength to fly the ancient pathways. They rely on the wisdom of the birds who preceded them. In return for their faith, they find forage and good nesting in beautiful surroundings.

The Canada Goose tells of the need to finish the pilgrimage of life, because it is the right thing to do. He champions the need to muster the strength to do what must be done, even if it is difficult, and despite what any group tells you. You must choose what is right over what is convenient, and sometimes, what is popular. You know, in your soul, what must be the correct path.

The reverse of the card warns of the pitfalls of ethical instability, both moral and emotional. It is not just your life that is affected, the lives of the clan are also touched. You must guard against devotion to compulsion and obsession.

Brown Bear

CHOICES, DECISIONS, OPTIONS

Brown Bear ranges far and wide, sampling the pleasures of life. He has learned life is an experience to be savored and shared. Of a generous nature, Brown Bear has bestowed many great gifts upon humanity, and he is honored as the symbol of choices, decisions, and options.

You may not have the choices you would like, but you have more than you may believe. You must face your decisions as a matter not only of survival but of living well. Your options are to remain in situations of others' making or to go forward and recreate yourself and your life. The real decision is figuring out what the best choice is for you and yours. Are you chasing the future or a pleasant dream with no basis in reality? Dreams can come true, but at a price; and reality is rarely as easily managed as fantasy.

The reverse of the card indicates the lack of recognition of options or choices and poor decision making. Learn to understand that some decisions require research, and some decisions can only be made by intuition. Use your head and follow your heart.

Black Bear

INTROSPECTION, SELF-ANALYSIS

Black Bear is reserved, even shy, but friendly. He will never hurt anyone purposely, but he will lash out if he is frightened or mightily provoked. Physically, he will do no harm unless his life or the lives of his family are in peril. He is a good mate and a loving, protective parent.

You will find Black Bear in places of tranquillity. He eschews environments where the pace is frantic and the stress is high. Though he avoids crowds, he is not always a recluse, and he will, sometimes, entertain a select few. He is very charming when he consents to socialize, and he is very amusing. Black Bear is more popular than he is interested in being, and after too short a time for his admirers, he disappears into his beloved solitude.

Black Bear's lessons are not a recommendation to act the hermit. Rather, he tells of the need to find places of quietude. Only in such places may you learn the arts Black Bear has mastered: introspection and self analysis.

Black Bear tells us that only these two gifts to ourselves will let us experience, even recognize the additional and wonderful gifts of great love, the enjoyment of having fun, and the joy of life. Further, they will help us accept that while we may not be able to understand hate, we can reject it without any need for explanation.

Remember, Black Bear urges, there are things that the introspective soul will understand that the person who has not experienced such self-analysis cannot. How to explain something that cannot be comprehended without experience? The answer is, Black Bear assures, to not explain. Simply enjoy life, and reject hate.

Wander the dense forest of experience not as an ascetic, but as a traveler who knows the truth is in his own soul. Follow Black Bear's counsel, stand back from your ego, and ask what everyone's motives (including your own) really are. Self-analysis is only useful when it is true, not merely self-reassurance or a farce of introspection.

Black Bear cherishes the uniqueness of each soul, he recognizes the talents of each clan member as important to both the group and the individual. Change your attitudes, be more generous and more circumspect.

The appearance of Black Bear signifies a desire for introspection and self-analysis. Stop and listen to yourself, do not fear the words of your soul. Leave the frenzy for a while so you can hear.

Black Bear cautions, however, that you must not become so enamored of the process that you forget to forge ahead and achieve. Introspection is not an excuse for immobility. Rather, it and self-analysis are part of the preparation needed for forward motion. Face change and live life to the fullest.

The reverse of the card indicates a lack of introspection and a need for self-analysis. Do you act or react? What are your motives and goals. Do you need to examine your motives and establish clear goals?

Grizzly Bear

STRESS, TENSION, LACK OF SYNCHRONICITY

Grizzly Bear is formidable indeed. He can be a dangerous creature, moody and unpredictable as well as magnificent and strong. When he lays claim to anything, he defends it with great vigor and ferocity. He will also defend his family to the death. Grizzly Bear mother is beyond formidable, and her protective instincts border on obsession.

Grizzly Bear, male or female, does not share territory easily, preferring independence and solitude. It is best to remember who is ruler when roaming the kingdom of the Great Bear.

While the potential for danger is obvious, Grizzly Bear is not as unpredictable as many believe. He is curious and alert, always aware of his surroundings. He investigates, he learns and draws conclusions. Sometimes, he reaches the wrong conclusion, and that is when the problems occur.

Grizzly Bear is good at recognizing danger, his keen instincts are honed to knife-edge sharpness. This kind of alertness generates tension, and that generates stress. This is not negative, but chemistry that enables Grizzly Bear to react with lightning speed and neutralize the danger.

Sometimes, Grizzly Bear overreacts and sees danger where there is little threat, or rages at a causal incident as though it were a great affront. This only happens when the situation is one that is new and strange to Grizzly, so it is best to go slow until he is accustomed to the change. He will embrace change, but only after he gets to know it.

Because of his powerful body and mind, mankind has recognized the Spirit of the Bear as one of great power and blessing. Grizzly has always gifted those who are respectful and observant with the blessing of knowledge.

When Grizzly comes to you, he tells you of change that you must accept slowly, and on your own terms. He speaks of stress and tension, danger in allowing the situation to get to you and eat you away. Gain knowledge, ask questions, do not rush in until you understand what is happening.

Beware allowing yourself to permit life to scatter itself at a time when synchronicity matters most. Avoid seeing threats that are little more than annoyances, allowing stress to become an illness instead of tool for survival. Determine what is a real danger, not just an uncomfortable but necessary change. You must deal with real threats head on, armed with knowledge and understanding. You must face change, head held high, knowing change is not a threat.

The reverse of this card indicates someone who does not know when to stand his ground. There are times when the power of the Grizzly Bear is to be used, but with common sense and control.

Polar Bear

AGGRESSION, NOT SEEING OPTIONS

A sparkling white coat, great paws, and an appealing face make Polar Bear a visual delight. In addition, his nature can be most congenial. Never forget, however, Polar Bears are fierce predators, dangerous under the best circumstances, and not to be taken lightly no matter how attractive they appear. They can be very playful and may appear very sweet, but they are never tame nor is there ever a time when they are not dangerous. They are highly specialized hunters, unable to vary their habits, even when faced with a dearth of prey. Rather than adapt to unexpected conditions, or learn new techniques, they will starve to death.

The resolute adherence to tradition the Polar Bear embodies must be balanced by adaptability. You must survive, you must be sure that those dependent upon you also survive.

Polar Bear has all the charm of his kind as well as all the talents, and a special insight. When he comes to you, he is telling you of a person too enmeshed in the past, so impressed with the way things are done, he cannot accept repatterning. Aggression must be controlled. The excuse of threat or temptation must not be used. Anger will blind you, and your spirit will melt like ice in the summer.

When Polar Bear speaks to you, you must take a deep breath and face yourself. Who is this aggressive soul who has closed his or her eyes to the many options and the advantages change can bring? First, determine whether or not it is you. If not, is it someone you love and hope will change?

No one can change without wanting to do so, and no one can be changed by another. Education and self-discipline are the only tools you have. Encouragement and a refusal to accept the dark side of aggression are the only gifts you can give one another.

Enthusiasm can replace aggression; it can be life's blood rather than hot blood. Respecting tradition while progressing as a free soul can replace being so bound by tradition that your spirit starves until you are only a shell, preforming daily functions, waiting for the grave.

The reverse of this card tells of someone out of control. You must respect history, not abandon it nor be enslaved. You must stop the winter storm of anger, of aggressive behavior. You must use aggressive tendencies to effect positive change, not to try to force issues.

If the person out of control is one who would control others, including you, then you must escape. Escape is not desertion. However, you must not allow yourself, or anyone who is vulnerable and within your grasp, to be the victim of the white rage. There is a time to stand your ground, and a time to leave. No one can stand up to the power of the Polar Bear out of control, you must refuse to be a victim. Your suffering is the chain that binds you to the one causing your suffering, and your spirits will surely die sad, unnecessary deaths unless chaos is transformed to order.

Turtle

RELIABILITY, INSTINCTUAL TRUST

Turtle is the citizen of a nation with many tribes and a staggering array of clans. Some clans are fierce warriors, like the magnificent snapping turtle, others are more content to go about their business, like the handsome Terrapin. All share the same sense of honor, dedication, and reliability that marks the Turtle as a blessed being, a favorite of the Great Spirit.

In legend, it is said life owes its movement to the Great Turtle who travels through the Universe with slow, steady steps as the dance of existence is performed on his back. He is revered as the soul of ultimate stability and reliability. Further, he is revered as the sign and symbol of those virtues. Turtle is also honored as a sign to trust in one's own instincts. The Turtle knows when to stick his neck out to make progress, and when to pull that neck, as well as the rest of himself, into his sturdy shell. He observes life quietly, with a gimlet eye and good sense. No one fools the Turtle; he can hear truth as a song, and he can detect a wrong note so faint few others will ever hear it. He listens to the soul as well as the words. He does his research, he finds the facts, and he weighs them against what he has observed.

Turtle counsels you that instincts are less psychic than they are observation. Drawing conclusions based on fact, real fact not prejudice, leads to good instincts. You can educate your instincts, and enhance the psychic ability by increasing your analytical ability. No snap decisions here, only calm, cool assessment.

When Turtle comes to you, he speaks of the need to be reliable and to be in the company of those who are reliable. He tells you, too, that you must trust in your instincts and observe among your associates which of them have instincts to be trusted.

Do not indulge, Turtle warns, in the luxury of decisions based on whim. Change rarely comes at breakneck speed, it plods along like the turtle, steady and unwavering. A poor decision made now may be impossible to correct later.

The reverse of this card warns of unreliability in a crucial place. Do not ignore the intuition of the turtle spirit. Be reliable, and record your efforts. Turtle carries the record of his life on his shell, he warns you to keep a record of your actions in an equally safe, accessible place. Trust in the plenitude of nature, and be aware of the fickle nature of man. Do not assume everyone will do what is right even as you strive to remain, like Turtle, ethical.

Beaver

EFFORT, INDUSTRY, PROGRESS

No creature can boast the accomplishments of Beaver. Efficient effort, learned industry, and unrelenting progress towards established goals are the hallmarks of this spirited soul. Beaver chooses his location carefully, decides what is to be done, and then how it will be accomplished.

Beaver is a sign of intelligent success. Beaver is also a sign of things finished and new projects to be started. Beaver and his fellow workers will build their amazing dwellings, refurbishing and adding until they become so perfect that the pond is altered, dried, and becomes a fertile meadow after generations have passed.

Family is very important to Beaver. He is a loyal and true mate, and a devoted parent. His young are welcome to stay and learn until they are thoroughly schooled in the art of the family business. Often, his young will stay in the family enclave, helping with the business, and eventually, taking it as their own. One of Beaver's great secrets is his ability to foment cooperative efforts, coordinate group industry, and establish goals that satisfy the needs of the family and community.

Beaver can also be narrow-minded concerning his devotion to conformity, insisting on doing things in the traditional manner even if those methods are not best suited to the situation. He can, and will sometimes, learn new things, if they are introduced slowly and in manageable doses. In a crisis situation, however, he becomes amazingly adaptable, definitely thinking past the traditional. Do not think the revolution won, though, for often Beaver will revert to the ways of his ancestors, discarding the new survival techniques.

Beaver comes not only to tell you of the effort and industry necessary to accomplish your goals, he may also tell you the goal is accomplished and that it is time to begin anew. However tradition bound, he does know when the job is done.

The reverse of this card tells of those who would impede your progress, counseling you to use your energy for their purposes. Do not become the instrument of their aggrandizement at the expense of yourself or the community. Effort and industry are goals worthy of you only when they are constructive and ethical.

Beaver knows that life is subject to the ebb and flow of change, as surely as the water overtakes or releases the land. It is nothing to be feared, only dealt with. He councils us to revere our traditions, but to understand that traditions become chains when they weigh us down in prejudice, impede our growth, and cause us to be cruel or to turn away from those we should love. Progress toward our goals is not discarding the old, it is taking the beautiful, the spiritual, and the love with us as we create new traditions for ourselves.

Wolverine

PERSISTENCE, EXTRA EFFORT

Wolverine looks as if he may be a member of the bear clan, or perhaps the badger, but he is the largest of the weasel tribe. Unlike his smaller cousins, he is not blessed with sleekness and swift skills. He is not troubled, however, by what he does not have, he knows that his talents more than make up for what he lacks.

Wolverine is a fierce creature, the toughest fighter anyone will meet. He is admired for his tenacity, his refusal to abandon what he believes is right.

He brings that same persistence to every part of his life. Once he has established his goal, Wolverine will work tirelessly to bring about its realization, no matter how much energy is needed. He is the very symbol of the extra effort it takes to effect necessary change and the persistence it takes to maintain positive change.

Wolverine gives to us the strength and power to resist negativity. He assures us that we can overcome anything if only we will put forth the effort needed. He reminds us that we need to be able to work on our own, and that we need to be able to work as part of a team.

Wolverine is willing to build on the success of others. He is less worried about who gets the kudos than he is interested in getting the job done so that everyone may reap the rewards. He is not timid about joining a project, lending his talents, and improving on the idea.

He tells you to watch for invitations to join good projects. It may be a subtle hint or disguised as a joke. Remember no one likes rejection, and some will not take the chance of being rejected. If a hint is cast in your direction, take it with the joyful fierceness of Wolverine. Hasten to contribute your talents as well as take part in the victory.

What if, you ask, it was not an invitation, perhaps it was just a joke. Then, says Wolverine, all that has happened is that you have made it known you are a team player as well as an individual. More than likely, he tells you with a wink, you have opened the proverbial door of change to better not only your life, but theirs.

The reverse of this card indicates a lack of persistence. The effort is worth making, but falling into negativity is easier than making positive change. Take your cue from the wolverine, a determined creature. What is there to fear? What have you to lose? Work on your interpersonal skills. The idea that Wolverine is an unpleasant creature and destructive is simply misunderstanding. Wolverine is not here to tell you to be nasty and wreak havoc, he is here to tell you to go forth and get that which you have dreamed of having. Change the perceptions people have that you are a loner and that you will not or cannot progress. You can do it, Wolverine will show you how.

Blue Heron

HOPE, POSITIVE ATTITUDE

A stately creature of land, water, and air, Blue Heron symbolizes hope as well as a positive attitude. Ever resourceful and patient, he walks through the water alert to the possibilities. A powerful bird, he floats upon the air currents from place to place, accepting nature's gifts.

He does not rely entirely on the largess of luck, however, in order to live. He trusts in nature's bounty, but he realizes he has to go out and look for it, too. Blue Heron is skilled at finding opportunities where there seem to be none. He is a problem solver, a thinker who considers not what has always been done, but how to approach the situations that change has brought.

He takes his hopes and then creates an environment that will allow them to come to fruition. If the bounty of the water is less than sufficient, he will look to the land. If the place he has always nested is no longer satisfactory, he will take to the skies and find a better spot.

Blue Heron nests in high places that are comfortable, convenient, and protected, be it a stately tree or a cozy roof. He has learned to accept and benefit from human invaders, and they look upon his presence as a sign of favor and luck. He is so admired that few will disturb his nest, hoping instead, that he will favor them with his presence and blessings every year.

One reason for the admiration Blue Heron enjoys is that Herons are creatures of family and families. If young Heron learning to live on his own cannot make it back to his parents' nest, he has nothing to fear. Any Blue Heron will accept him and feed him until he is able to try life on his own again. Everyone needs a little help sometimes.

Blue Heron comes to you with positive counsel and words of great importance. Further, Blue Heron brings the hope and positive attitude he symbolizes. He affirms the truth of hope and the determination needed to maintain a positive attitude. Do not waver, no matter how daunting your circumstances. The Blue Heron tells you this trouble, too, shall pass. It is not a cliche, it is truth.

The reverse of Blue Heron's card cautions you against falling into the morass of self-pity created by hopelessness and negative attitudes. Gather the skills, education, and information you need, but be wary of doing more than considering the opinions of others. Too often opinions are advice, and advice is expected to be taken. No one has to live with the results but you. If it is advice you are seeking, look into your own heart. You can be victim of the attitudes of others, but you are, in this case, more likely the victim of your own attitudes.

White Tail Deer

DEVOTION, PERSONAL SACRIFICE, SELFLESSNESS

Is there a more magical creature than Deer? From the dawn
of time, Deer has been the symbol of soulful beauty, devotion and sacrifice. Deer has given his very life so that other
creatures, including man, might survive. It is the symbol of
personal sacrifice, benefitting others without want of
reward, glory, or gratitude.

Legends tell us Deer has chosen to sacrifice life for
others, without compromising ethics or conscience. Further,
he preserves the "self" even when he gives up his life. A
noble being, Deer considers all the options before making a

decision. Grandiose, empty sacrifices are unworthy of so soulful a being as Deer.

Deer is not only generous, but teaches generosity. He is devoted to his family, his community, and the world. His is the sign of a devoted friend and partner, asking for nothing in return, but often receiving much.

There is a genuine inquisitiveness that is part of Deer's nature. His pursuit of answers can sometimes lead him into danger; it can sometimes cause him to overlook other concerns. There are times when he seems to suffer ill consequences resulting from his investigations, but Deer tells us the lack of knowledge is certainly worse. He also says that lessons he has learned are to be passed to others so that they may use the knowledge and build upon it.

When Deer steps from the shadows and speaks to you, he tells you that you will be called upon to honor your feelings and promises of devotion as he does. You will find that you will be stronger spiritually as you perform to benefit others, even at personal sacrifice. Deer admonishes you to always remember to be selfless, but not a victim. You are not to be a ritual sacrifice or an offering to someone else's greed. You must choose worthy beneficiaries of your largess, and once chosen, you must sacrifice.

The reverse of this card cautions you to be like the noble Deer, not a target. Deer can run, Deer can fight, Deer survives as a population. You must learn when to say yes and when to say no. Then you must learn to maintain your resolve, stand by your word, and go on. The winds of change are not to be feared.

Turkey

LUCK, HAPPINESS,
IMPROVEMENT IN FORTUNE

The Wild Turkey is a sleek bird, intelligent and artful. He is admired by those who know him and he ignores the opinions of the ignorant. Turkey takes pride in his skills and enjoys his life.

Self-confident, but very reserved, Wild Turkey was a favorite of the Aztecs. In 1500, four of his ancestors were purchased for the impressive sum of four fine glass beads each. They were taken to Europe where they were known as d'Inde in Spain and dindon in France, both referring to his Native American admirers. Europeans, too, held the bird they called the "Turk" in high esteem, and he became as popular in the Old World as in the New.

Wherever Wild Turkey has walked, good fortune has followed. It is no surprise to his admirers that he has been immediately adopted as the symbol of happiness and better things to come.

Wild Turkey comes to tell you that you are about to enter a period of fortuitous circumstances. Things will go your way if you follow the path with your eyes open and your skills sharp. Be sure you have updated your skills, that you have kept yourself in top condition. You will need mind, body, and soul to accept the changes that are coming. You will also need to look deep into yourself and discover what your really want. Whatever your dreams are, many, if not all, are about to be offered to you.

Wild Turkey has good counsel for you as well as grand announcements. Happiness comes to those who fly the path of their dreams while helping others. Improvement in fortune comes to the one who is alert to opportunity and who creates opportunity. Like the wily turkey, keep your wits about you, and do not panic. The day will be won by the patient and the bold. Enthusiasm is warranted, hysteria is not. Maintain a sense of reservation and dignity, but not an air of arrogance or a lack of appreciation.

The reverse of this card warns of someone who has become complacent and too domestic. The comfort enjoyed may have a very high price when the debt must be repaid. Happiness comes from striving, contentment is attained in achievement. Look at each opportunity with clear eyes. See what is best for you and judge what is a good opportunity to give to someone else. There is much coming to you, more than you can possibly accept. Be generous.

Mule Deer

LACK OF KNOWLEDGE, UNCERTAIN FUTURE,
UNFORSEEN CIRCUMSTANCES

Mule Deer is often considered gregarious and one who fol-
lows the crowd. However, closer examination reveals that
he tends toward solitude and he moves in small groups,
usually with family connections. Family is the one true loyalty for the Mule Deer. He is a good friend, but family
always comes first. Because of this, Mule Deer avoids form-
ing friendships, and he is very discriminating. Most of his
friends are, like him, very family oriented.

As a group, nuclear or extended family, Mule Deer is
a symbol of the lack of knowledge. This is more a reflec-

tion of man's ignorance than any shortcoming of the deer. Their future is cloudy because of the human tribe. They understand their world as it is, only man denies what is possible and real.

Mule Deer steps forward to explain to you the significance and the full scope of where the lack of knowledge can lead and how a cloudy future can be the result. Refusing to consider the complete picture can cause an unending ripple throughout not only your life, but the lives of all those around you.

Mule Deer tells you to always remember all knowledge is precious and your pursuit of it must be fleet. You will survive, as the Mule Deer survives in some of the harshest environments known to humans, and you will find yourself in a beautiful place filled with hard won bounty. All the harshness will be behind you.

Some anxiety is to be expected, but do not let your nerves work themselves into full grown terrors, unseen and unknown, such that you are unable to pounce. You must face the future with a plan, not fear. You must consider all of your options, and understand what can result from your actions.

The reverse of this card warns of what the refusal to gather facts will cost you. Your future can be lost, as seeds on dry sand. This can be averted, but it is in your hands. You may have to stand and fight, or you may have to run from a bad situation just as a mule deer flees danger he cannot stand against and survive. Ignore the opinions of others who would use their imagined superiority to deride you or dissuade you. Mule Deer knows when to stand his ground and when to retire into the forest. Use your own good judgement. None of your detractors are going to step forth and save you, they will only criticize you more.

Mountain Goat

STEADY PROGRESS, UPWARD MOBILITY

Mountain Goat is a glorious creature, actually an antelope related to the Chamois of Europe. His name is a tribute to the intelligence and tenacity traits he shares with his very distant relative. He lives in territory so rugged it is difficult to believe any creature can survive, much less thrive. But thrive he does. Mountain Goat achieves success by means of steady progress and stalwart attention to meaningful detail.

Mountain Goat has strong family and community values. He shoulders responsibility as quickly as he joins in fun. He keeps his eye on his goals, and he watches for changes that may affect his progress. Mountain Goat does not consider change the enemy, simply a factor to take into account.

Mountain Goat is the symbol of upward mobility. He has come to tell you that his life is an analogy for your progress. Mountain Goat leads the herd higher each summer, dining upon tender shoots and twigs, enjoying air so pure it is intoxicating. It is a path that is not only physical, but psychic and metaphysical as well. He counsels you to walk the same psychic and metaphysical path. In doing so, you will attain the rarefied heights you seek.

Not all of your journey will be spiritual or intellectual. Some of it will be just as physical as those mountain paths. Be ready with a steady hand and quick foot. Keep your wits about you, one misstep can send you tumbling down the cliff side for an inglorious landing. Mountain Goat tells you not to be afraid. He rarely falls and when he does, it amounts to very little. He just shakes himself clean and dashes back up the mountain's side. You, too, will just dust yourself off and launch yourself again. The glory can be won again. In fact, it's more fun to do it over again.

The reverse of Mountain Goat's card tells of a stagnant, stubborn refusal to climb out of the cold shadows to see the blue skies and feel the warm sun. Sitting in the dark has its place, but not here. Mountain Goat is here to tell you to stop moping and get up, get to it and get going.

Rabbit

SENSITIVITY, ORGANIZATION

Charming and resourceful, Rabbit makes his way through a world filled with beautiful flowers. He dines on the finest vegetation and drinks the sweet, clean water. Rabbit is alert and has the talent to make sound decisions right on the spot. The reason why he can do this is that he considers possible alternatives, and he remains flexible in his thinking. He also maintains himself physically, staying in top condition and avoiding anything that might slow or impede his abilities to fulfill his tasks.

The appearance of Rabbit is the advent of great strides achieved through change. He is a creature of special heart and magic, as well as a social being with a talent for organization. Rabbit is the sign of one sensitive to many things, including the feelings of others.

There is another side to rabbit. He can be willful and wily. There are times when he puts his desires ahead of the legitimate needs of others. He will do this, even after being counseled against such actions by those he respects. He regrets the exploitation, upon reflection, and is willing to apologize as well as make amends, but it is usually only after he has suffered some cosmic punishment for misusing his talents. The punishment is always a direct result of his own actions, so there is no mistaking the message.

When Rabbit comes to you, it is in the dual role of the selfless and the selfish. He speaks of regrets that are empty without redress. He speaks of a necessity for sensitivity to the needs of others. He also urges you to listen to yourself concerning your own needs. He wishes to teach you important lessons and to help you make an urgent change. Rabbit has come to give you a great gift: the realization that all living creatures have feelings that must be considered as important as your own. Part of the gift is also realizing that your feelings are important.

Rabbit understands that such new realizations and new concepts require great changes. He comes to you to aid you in your tasks. He will inspire you to become organized in your quest to meet the needs you face. You do not need to burrow deep into some dark place to achieve the new quest. Contrary to popular opinion, Rabbit rarely burrows. He lives near the earth, taking advantage of the shelter the land gives him, and enjoying the cool twilight of the setting sun. You need to go forth into the fresh air of life, not bury yourself.

The reverse of Rabbit's card indicates a stubborn lack of sensitivity and a lack of organization, both of which will become a wall of overpowering weight. You must resist the temptation to fall into disorganization and chaos. This is not the time to indulge yourself.

Mouse

LOSS, SOMETHING MISSING

Mouse slips through the house, taking not only food but little shiny things back to the nest. To him, golden colored foil is just as precious as a golden ring; it is a matter of viewpoint, and Mouse a has perspective that is uniquely his own. He is the wise grandparent, he knows much and he will share it, but only if you are patient. He is eccentric because he knows the ways of the world, seen and unseen.

Mouse understands priorities and goals. He knows food and shelter are most important; survival is the goal. However, Mouse is prone to consider all uses of his time, outside of the tasks needed for survival, as equally important. Work that must be accomplished is overlooked in favor of finishing routine chores that can be delayed once in the while or even delegated to others. Mouse is intelligent, and he realizes that something is out of sync when he is busy all the time, but accomplishing little of importance.

Know that Mouse is also a teacher. Once he realizes something is out of sync or missing, he will set about rectifying the situation. He is a loving but demanding grandparent, a guardian of good manners, and one who chides those who waste opportunities or available resources.

The human holding the card of Mouse is one who has experienced loss and feels something important is missing in his life. Like Mouse, he or she is on the go constantly, but getting nowhere. Mouse tells you to assess your situation before making changes, but know that changes still must be made.

What has life taken from you that you need to take back? Have you lost opportunities? If so, Mouse tells you to find new ones. Have you missed out on experiences? Mouse tells you to count the experiences you have had, and find new experiences.

The reverse of this card tells you of a blithe ignorance of what you are missing. You have overlooked the thief that time can be, and you must understand that now is the moment to take action.

Caribou

MEDITATION, THOUGHT

Caribou is the symbol of all things good. He is also the sign of thought, as well as equality. Buck or Doe, Caribou is crowned with great, solid antlers and blessed with a steady step. So sure is Caribou's gait, he can traverse wide expanses of ice and snow as easily as soft grass of summer.

Steady, too, is Caribou when faced with change. He thinks, he meditates, and he bases his decisions on observation as well as insight and intuition. He grazes the tundra and considers his surroundings as well as his life. Caribou gives thought to what may be on the horizon, and waits to see whether or not it is dangerous. He does not panic just because something is new, but he values discretion.

Caribou is a sign of family; he participates fully in the survival of the entire family. He can be relied upon during the worst of times, and he is always welcomed at the best of times. He does not seek to seize control or trumpet his abilities; he works quietly, efficiently and kindly to make any situation better, even if he will not benefit directly.

His is a life of simple pleasures and sweet joys. Good food, friends, and family are enough; he likes his life plain. Caribou does not worry himself or anyone else into anxiety induced stress episodes. Stress, for Caribou, is a signal of danger, and the adrenaline it inspires is used as creative energy. It is not wasted on worry.

Drawing the card of the Caribou tells you to take time to evaluate a situation. Do not worry about the effects or aftershocks of any problem until after you have identified the problem and the source. Sometimes, you will discover the difficulty is only the perception of change as some faceless enemy, not just part of the process of living. Meditate upon your situation and ask yourself how much of your reaction is based on vague feeling and how much on fact. Ask yourself how much control you really have over any situation and consider that you, like Caribou, may need to do nothing more than adapt.

The reverse of this card is a failure to meditate. To meditate is to concentrate on what your soul is trying to tell you, what the Universe wants you to know. It is the failure to respect your own thought. After all, if you cannot give yourself that respect, how can you respect another or be respected by others?

Hummingbird

INSIGHT AND ENJOYMENT OF LIFE

Living among the flowers in some of the most beautiful places in the world, including your backyard, Hummingbird is a joy to behold and joy incarnate. His is the career of living. Humming Bird is also the sign of the spirit and the sacred. He takes nourishment from beauty and nourishes beauty.

With all the wonderful things Hummingbird represents, remember one very important thing: he can fly backwards. Hummingbird is a master at negotiating flight lanes filled with obstacles of all kinds, and there are times when he flies backwards. There are times when you need to rethink your path. New facts and new attitudes should not be ignored, changing your flight plan is not a sign of weakness, it is, rather, the sign of the lively mind of Hummingbird.

Seek to enjoy your life, including the flight toward your goals. Seek to learn from each experience as though it were a flower of nourishment. No matter if it is the sweet and exotic hibiscus or the everyday, homey honey-suckle, each has the nectar of insight you need. Remember, also, to consider your soul and the souls of others; return the favor of survival by preserving that which is truly beautiful, not just cosmetic.

Watch your health and the health of those around you. Your community of human and animal loves must be in top condition for this journey. Release your fears and fly.

The reverse of this card is a warning of failing to learn from experience and failing to take the joy offered. There is a time for caution and for mourning. This is not it.

Otter

AID, HELP, CREATIVITY

Sleek and true, Otter is an individual, smart and skillful. Even as a child, Otter is independent and always running. Otter is resourceful and creative, he can think of more ways to solve a problem in a moment than others can conjure in a week. What's more, most of the solutions will work well.

Otter tends to work alone, and he is content in solitude. However, he is always helpful and willing to aid anyone in need. His is a generous soul.

Because of his gracious and innovative nature, Otter often symbolizes man in legends. His is also the form chosen by helpful spirits when they come to the rescue.

Otter gives aid in the form of information and action. He is the image of the proactive teacher. He instructs his students while he works with them, shoulder to shoulder.

The arrival of Otter speaks of the need to seek aid from those with knowledge and understanding. Otter also urges helping others as you would be helped yourself. He cautions you that the Universe returns sevenfold or more what you give. Send out the warmth of one who stands ready to help, one who will come to anyone's aid, and you will reap the rewards of a true heart and generous spirit. Otter knows this, and he tells you to take it into your soul.

Even more importantly, Otter shows you the path to your creativity. Consider how you have solved problems in the past, ask yourself what you have learned and what you need to do differently. Learn from experience, do not be enslaved by habit. Now is the time to change for the better. Change will come, you cannot stop it, but you can face it with a renewed spirit and a new attitude. Otter is your guide, you cannot fail.

The reverse of Otter's card warns of an unwillingness to accept aid when offered, a refusal to help for fear of being criticized. It can also symbolize a stifling of creativity. Do not close your mind to Otter's tender counsel. Know he speaks for the Universe, he is of water and earth, a sacred soul who is a chosen one. Listen and learn, let your heart absorb the lessons.

Opossum

AVOIDANCE, RESISTANCE TO IDEA,
OPPOSING POINTS OF VIEW

Opossum is a marsupial, related to a group of animals including the kangaroo. He is something of a walking fossil; a slow-thinking soul with unusually adaptable characteristics. Never underestimate Opossum, however, for his origins are ancient and he has survived where others have not. Those who think slowly also think carefully, and those who think carefully not only survive, but live well.

He is a good planner and he knows what he is going to do under any circumstance. Do not be fooled into thinking he is ever inert; he is wide awake and watching for an opportunity. He knows change in circumstances are inevitable and he waits for his opening. He really is only "playing possum" to avoid confrontation.

Opossum reminds you to avoid confrontation. What will confrontation bring you? Should you stand your ground or retreat silently?

Opossum has more lessons for you. There is a warning about resisting ideas and ignoring other points of view. Opossum reminds you that you are not programmed to react a certain way, and if you insist on acting as if you are, there is no second chance if that program is not successful. Are you playing possum to avoid a situation over which you have no control? Or are you playing possum because it is comfortable? Are you discarding different ideas because they have no merit? Or because they are not your ideas and they interfere with your pleasant world? Are you refusing to consider other points of view because they are invalid and hurtful? Or do they make you uncomfortable because you might have to do something to right a wrong?

Remember, however, there will always be opposing points of view; just because you are not always right, that does not mean you are always wrong. You can learn to tell the difference between acting as if you were an automaton because you were always told you could not help your self or change, and acting like the free-willed, spirited fighter you really are. Do you think Opossum a homely soul? No, he is humble, but noble and good. Look past the myths and the stories, particularly look past the misinformation and truths that are really falsehoods. Look past appearance, and behold both Opossum and yourself, children of the gods.

Remember Opossum's lessons and do not avoid change, embrace it. Do not fear confrontation, manage it so it becomes a lively exchange of ideas, a way to build a future. Those you would perceive as enemies because they disagree are often merely people with a different point of view. Listen, learn, speak, teach; that is Opossum's wise counsel.

The reverse of the card warns you that you may be too confrontational. You are too willing to fight for the sake of fighting, not for what is right. Instead of considering the ideas of others along with your own, you discard your own out of self-doubt. You are drawn to opposing points of view because they are glamorous, not because they have merit. That is not the way of earthy Opossum. He is not fooled, he knows truth. Learn.

Peregrine Falcon

SURVIVAL, ADAPTABILITY,
OVERCOMING OBSTACLES

Snatched from the brink of extinction, Peregrine Falcon's clan is legendary for its ability to not only survive but adapt. Once, it built its nests in the rocky clefts of mountains; now it can be found raising its young on the ledges of high rises in the center of great cities.

Over the centuries, Peregrine Falcon was welcomed in the homes of Europeans and Middle Easterners. He was admired for his beauty and abilities. In North America, Peregrine Falcon was equally admired. He was also recognized for his spirituality.

However easily he may adapt to others and how comfortable he is with change, Peregrine Falcon has retained his regal and wild nature. He maintains the core of his personality, the purity of his soul under all circumstances. His adaptability and ability to overcome obstacles are survival skills. Nothing has changed his ethics or his good character.

Peregrine Falcon is a devoted mate and an attentive parent. He is a good teacher as well as an excellent student. He learns for the joy of learning, and he passes not only his knowledge but his respect for education onto his students whether they are his children or souls he has taken under his wing.

Peregrine Falcon comes to tell you that to survive you must learn how to adapt. Overcoming your obstacles is not as much a matter of luck as it is persistence and knowledge. Sometimes you need an obstacle to stand atop. If no craggy cliff face presents itself, then find a skyscraper to launch your dreams. Adaptability is not compromise of ethics unless you make it so.

A sterling example of tolerance, Peregrine Falcon urges you to accept others, even if they are different, and to judge others on the basis of what they do, not who they are. Peregrine Falcon does not preach dependence, his independence is too precious to compromise, and so should your independence be. He does tell you that your survival is united with the survival of others.

The reverse Peregrine Falcon's card tells you of an inability to face what is needed for your survival and that of the ones who depend upon you. Like the Peregrine Falcon, sometimes help is needed. Do not resist the honestly offered hand, there is no loss of dignity to accepting aid. The repayment is to pass the kindness to another in need.

Black Footed Ferret

Black Footed Ferret is a member of the weasel family and native to North America. He has many talents and quite a few eccentricities.

On one hand, he is a shameless poacher. On the other, he has shared many pleasant hours in the households of human as a beloved friend. It must be remembered that he is never tame. Those who would convince Ferret to be a part of their lives must understand he is relentless in everything he does.

Ferret pursues work and play with near obsessiveness. He plays to win, and he works to succeed. However, his concept of success may be very different from what others might expect.

Black Footed Ferret possesses a quick and lively mind. His entire being is curiosity. He stands for the search for truth, not that which is popularly acceptable, but real and right. Answers, not platitudes, are needed for the investigator who embodies this blessed creature.

He comes to you to instruct that it is time for you to search for what you need. There are truths you must find, and answers you must have. Too, you must now tell truths others need, and you must give answers they deserve. The time for little lies and polite misdirection is over. Circumstances are already changing. The truth you want, and the answers you need can no longer be hidden, and you can no longer hide.

Ferret does not wish you to expose your private secrets, he tells you not to strip your soul bare. Even as you read this, even as you hear his words, you know what the Universe is telling you. This change is like fresh air and sunshine streaming through a room kept dark for too long. The toxic, stale air is being swept away.

Remember, Ferret counsels, there are secrets that are not to be shared, and truths that are to be dispensed like food for the soul. Learn the difference between prying and answers.

The reverse of this card warns to keep truth sacred and beware answers that are expedient and not correct. Do not gossip, or you will pay a harsh price. Bearing false witness is one of the greatest sins.

Buffalo

STRENGTH, APPROPRIATE ACTION

Buffalo is actually American Bison, a creature of rare individuality as well as community. He is definitely the product of the unique environment afforded by the New World. He thrived on the challenges presented by a raw, unforgiving environment, and took action to turn adversity into advantage. A survivor of remarkable crises, Buffalo stands as the symbol of what can be accomplished even when you are standing at the brink of oblivion.

The magnificent Buffalo is the standard of survival, the symbol of getting what you need. He is strength incarnate as both an individual as well as a member of a mighty society. The good life depends, Buffalo tells us, on both the individual and the group.

A creature of great stature, Buffalo's survival is not only brute strength, but the courage to stand strong in the face of adversity. He has the strength of his convictions, and stands shoulder to shoulder with his fellows. He stands strong in the face of adversity.

Buffalo is also a creature of appropriate actions. He urges you to be generous to everyone, including yourself. Buffalo understands all that is sacred, and he reminds us the Universe is generous. He turns away from people who are stingy, for they are frightened, and the fearful are dangerous. They fear, he knows, trusting themselves, others, and worst of all, the Universe.

A highly-acclaimed mentor who instructs in the ways of survival and the ways of the sacred, Buffalo teaches that you must strive to be fair and kind. Buffalo also reminds you to maintain high standards. The Universe offers you many gifts, you must accept them with wisdom and appreciation. Buffalo has set the example for us all, his generosity has been legendary and granted without reservation.

Buffalo, male or female, has the ability to change his outlook in order to better facilitate a plan of appropriate action under any circumstance. He can be a creature of great emotion, but he cautions allowing your emotions to override your intellect, as your instinct is a dangerous way to live. As a teacher, he not only accepts the traits of personality that make us individuals, he makes allowances for those traits.

Drawing Buffalo's card is counsel to avail yourself of the resources at hand. Use your resources, including your own strengths and energies, creatively. Use however much you need, but do not waste yourself or what you have available to you. Do not squander your assets, employ them wisely, and they will increase rather than diminish with use. Act as both a student and a teacher, as both you will learn. Be pleased by your virtues, accept your faults rather than deny them, then work to change. Do not confuse indulgences with actual vice, no matter what society decides is the current label for anything.

The reverse of Buffalo's card tells of someone with great strength and fortitude, but one who may be accepting a version of truth that is without veracity. Stand strong for what is right, but make sure you have verified the facts yourself. Be wary of depending upon the word of someone else whose veracity may be unintentionally colored by their own concerns.

Horse

FREEDOM, CHARACTER, PERSONALITY

The beautiful inspiration for countless works of art, Horse is the breath of the wind; freedom on the hoof with an irrepressible personality. He is one of nature's finest creations, a masterpiece of grace and speed. Horse is one of the most universally admired creatures. It has been said Horse is not only gifted by the gods, but a gift of the gods.

Horse dances across the sands of history, the sign of his hoof being the emblem of change for everyone who marked his passing. Entire cultures have fallen before him only to rise again to greater glory with his help. No human civilization has ever attained the rarefied heights of glory without a written language and Horse. Horse is the physical form of change, of freedom. He is the personification of great character and the best of personality.

Honored as a representative of the four cardinal compass points, Horse reminds us we have choices. It is not necessary to spend your life walking in only one direction. Life, Horse tells us, is a circle, not a straight line. In fact, Horse wonders at those who simply plod along when they can ride wings of their visions, if only they would look up and see the light.

Even though Horse is an irrepressible individual, he also stands for the freedom to be found in cooperation. His community is the picture of solidarity and security without compromising freedom. Horse walks a path to wealth and community leadership, bringing glory to his community as well as his family and himself.

A creature of great intelligence as well as sharp instincts, Horse tells us that when we think we have all the answers, we have lost the ability to be wise. Horse is an explorer, he has seen every part of the world. He is adaptable, he changes his habits when he finds change will secure a better life. He sees failure as nothing more than a lesson that will help him achieve success.

The reverse of this card is to warn of threats to freedom, a willingness to compromise character, a weakness of personality that may have been brought upon by misfortune and self doubt. A citizen of the world, widely respected and admired, Horse urges you to take your place in your community. You have talents you don't even realize, talents that will bring you benefits as well as benefit others. Awaken your mind to new experiences, Horse advises. Reawaken your desires for exploration and education. Horse tells you to stop standing around rearing change, take charge and gallop right into a new and better life.

Lynx

SECRETS, TRUTH REVEALED

Lynx pads silently across the land, whether in summer forest or in winter snow, barely leaving a sign of his passage. Like the secrets of the soul, it keeps its own council. Each paw touches the earth and reveals something about the earth and the animal.

A nearly tireless explorer of his wide territories, Lynx rarely hurries. Nothing escapes his sharp observation, which is nearly mythological in reputation. Unlike most myths, this reputation is deserved.

Lynx considers what is before him, analyzes what he sees, pays attention to what he hears, and for him, truth opens itself like a flower beneath the sun. Secrets are as often truth ignored as confidences kept. Lynx does not pry, he is no gossip. The truths that come to him are truths worth knowing. They are life-giving and soul-nourishing, they are the blood of learning; wonderful things.

When you see the beautiful Lynx, his eyes shining like the sun's own fire, centered with cool, green emerald, listen rather than speak, see rather than look. Lynx warns you the secrets worth having litter your path like diamonds scattered across the forest floor. Take not just what you need, take what you want. This is education, this is the gift the Universe sends you with Lynx. Truth has been revealed to you, it is waiting for you to notice.

Lynx acknowledges there are some secrets and some truths purposely held. First, you must look into your own soul and ask if you have a right to those secrets. You cannot ask to share in the heart's dreams of others, you may only be invited. That is not a secret, it is private. You can only earn the honor, and realize it may never come. That is not a lack of love or respect, that is private. You know what you have a right to learn. Decide and ask. Lynx is swift and sure; what is his will be his.

Truths obscured are like curtains drawn, no one can see. Secrets that are yours to know, and have been long held silent, are going to be told. Do not expect your life to be the same, and beware cursing what you have learned. Lynx tells you life is a lesson, and truth long obscured when it is truth you need, can no longer be the mystery endured. There is no future without the past. Sweep away the mythology, the prejudice, the view, good or bad, based on opinion and not fact. Seek and find the truth.

Secrets universal, secrets personal, and secrets yours to have are the truth the Lynx means to reveal. He further counsels that you, too, will find it is time to tell the secrets another, a dear one, deserves to hear. The truth must be revealed, or there will be no learning, no sharing, no love, no friendship.

The reverse of this card speaks of truth twisted and secrets that should be held sacred, broken. Confidences are not secrets to be shared. There is no need to tell all in the name of truth, only those who are entitled to the secret are to be included.

Red Headed Woodpecker

RATIONALITY, SELF-RELIANCE

A beautiful creature who sometimes drums on wood for the sheer joy of sound, Red Headed Woodpecker is the image of rationality and self-reliance. She is a thoughtful soul, a problem solver who learns the skills she needs. She will give help and she will accept help, but she will never stand back and let someone else do all the work. Nor will she do all of the work. Red Headed Woodpecker knows that you cannot help someone build confidence if he or she is always told to stand on the side lines. That, she will tell you, is not the way to teach self-reliance or rational thought.

Her talents are many and she employs with a joyful heart. Red Headed Woodpecker is a skilled woodsman who drills the tree trunks with an even, alternating rhythm. She creates a fine home for her family in excellent wood, always located in an area that is both peaceful and bountiful.

She does not trust luck, however. A rational soul realizes that even the best plans can be shattered in a storm. Should anything happen to that home, Red Headed Woodpecker will take her eggs to another location, one already scouted before the mishap. Red Headed Woodpecker always has good insurance and plenty of resources available, like acorns cached in safes she has drilled in various trees.

Red Headed Woodpecker does not allow her children to eat only one food; there are times when that is not available. They are trained to cultivate their taste, to experiment as well as to be practical, and to think things out.

The attitude of Red Headed Woodpecker towards the philosophy of life and all that is spiritual is very much like the attitude toward work and family. She is a patient soul who relies on what is beneath the surface. The superficial is inadequate for the Red Headed Woodpecker, male or female. She teaches her children to make their decisions based on research and facts, not fanciful gossip.

Red Headed Woodpecker comes to tell of information needed, a lack of self-awareness and knowledge. You must learn to listen and rely upon yourself for satisfaction in life.

Woodpecker urges you to stop standing on the sidelines instead of joining in the work and play. Change, for you, is fresh air and sunny days; desert the drabness of what you cannot do, and do what you can. Learn what you can do; like the woodpecker, you will find yourself drumming for the sheer joy of accomplishment.

Like Red Headed Woodpecker, your knowledge and information will be shared. Once you have replaced emotional reaction with honest emotion and reason based on rationality and knowledge, you will find you will have moved to a position of adviser. You will not offer advice, you will be asked for it, and you will understand that the best advice is to look inside one's self. Self-reliance is the key to all things. It is inserted into the lock of self-doubt, so that the door to education and experience may be opened to the mind as well as the soul.

The reverse of this card is to warn that you are seeking answers and rationality from outside yourself. Do not give in to easy emotionalism. This defeats self-reliance, and therefore, defeats that part of you longing to accomplish something on your own. Learn the difference between using emotion as a mask that obscures what is really happening and true, valid emotion.

Remember, too, the lesson of Red Headed Wood Pecker: Relying on others, rather than cooperating with others, means you will never have something you can call your own.

Frog

PERSONAL GROWTH, PURSUIT OF GOALS

Frog is a member of a nation that is vast and varied. Each tribe of Frog is special, beautiful, and has its own colorful patterns. Each member of each tribe has his or her own talents and abilities. Frog's many tribes are examples of how diversity and difference are gifts of the universe. However, for all the diversity and difference, we see the variations are only that. For each national is, essentially, Frog. That is the greater gift of Frog and the Universe.

The mysteries of the Universe may be seen unfolding in the life of Frog. From egg to tadpole to adult, Frog is evolution itself. For that reason, we have long understood that

Frog is the messenger that the Universe has sent to tell us of personal growth as well as the pursuit of goals.

Frog tells you of the need to stretch past what you have achieved and what is familiar. As the tadpole who leaves the comfortable pool to venture as an adult upon the land, you will find greater challenge and rewards without having to give up the comfort of your original home. Set your goals outside of your current sphere, reach higher than you ever dared. Explore the possibilities, follow the dreams you dismissed as impossible.

Always understand that it is sameness that makes it possible to exchange ideas, but it is difference that leads to new ideas. Neither accept nor dismiss anything new just because it is new, whether it is an idea, a product, or another soul. Bring that same opinion to the traditional as well as the familiar.

Explore, research, understand, and most of all, see. What is there to learn that will lead to greater personal growth? What does the change, the introduction of what is new, or the reaffirmation of what is traditional, mean to you and to everyone around you? Does it aid goals or impede them? Is it your attitude that determines the staff or distaff? You will that find that impediments often result from attitude, not fact.

Frog tells you of a need for personal growth, a gnawing desire not fulfilled. Establishing goals and making positive changes are the seeds of that growth. Plant them in your fertile mind, water them with your soul's longing, tend them with your eager heart. Do not be dissuaded by others who fear change because they fear you will leave them or look at them with disdain. Reassure them, but stand firm. Change comes to us all, bidden or not. Things cannot stay as they were because life will not permit it. Join in life, and guide the progress in the direction you want to travel.

Otherwise, you will be carried along like a tadpole caught in a jar of water, trapped and at the mercy of whomever may, or may not, open the jar.

The reverse of this card is an admonishment to examine whether you should finish what you have started before starting anew. Is the project worth your while? Is the problem soluble in a way that is satisfactory? Within each problem you face are the seeds to its solution. The question is, should you even bother to solve it or should you simply learn to live with it?

Crow

INFORMATION, COMMUNICATION

Crow is an adaptable, intelligent creature able to learn from his environment and take advantage of resources. He brings messages of vital information and provides good counsel. When you see Crow, handsome, charming, playful and powerful, you see a beloved child of the Universe, an emissary of great status.

Ambassador Crow is the perfect blend of social grace and bravado. He is a skilled, fierce fighter; independent, yet very social. The always dashing Crow lives a grand life by his wits and many skills. He loves pretty things and good times.

Crow has the reputation of taking what belongs to others, and sometimes that is true. Since he trusts the Universe to provide, and it always has and has promised it always will, he does not consider that not everyone is so trusting. What he sees as fulfilling a need, whether it is giving something of his own or taking something that belongs to another, is sometimes a rude appropriation of property. In that respect, Crow is a bit of a scallywag.

Crow is sometimes careless about other's feelings, and he can be a terrible tease. However, he forms warm, fast friendships, even with those one might expect to be considered enemies. Moreover, Crow is a caring teacher who wants to make life better for everyone he can. Even in human legends where he is portrayed as a trickster and a scamp, Crow is still known as a bringer of knowledge, of information, and communication.

Crow instructs you to gather information to yourself. You must communicate with others, draw on their information, listen and consider their counsel before making your decision. You must sift through the information, separating fact from belief, solid conclusions from assumptions. Most importantly, Crow counsels, you must see what the information tells you about its sources.

Make no decision based on anything that is not fact. However, understand that even false facts, assumptions and gossip, are clues to how others think, what others will do, and of what they are, or are not, capable. When you learn about yourself, you learn about others. You learn about yourself by learning about others.

Crow tells you to guard your information; share it, but carefully, so that others are less likely to misconstrue it into something it is not. Learn to listen without comment unless you have real information to contribute. Learn to communicate, not just talk. Learn to hear communication, not just idle rambling. Learn to hear what is being said beneath the words.

When Crow comes to you, it is to tell you to listen, observe, and engage in real communication. Is someone trying to speak to you, and you aren't really listening? Are you trying to communicate, but no one is paying attention? Resolve to change either situation.

The reverse of this card is to understand that you must be careful about how much information you give. Are you sharing knowledge or gossiping? Are you teaching or bragging? Are you giving your enemies ammunition to use against you? The crow is wise and knows the power of words.

Ring Necked Pheasant

COMFORT, HARMONY, SATISFACTION,
ATTAINING GOALS

Carried from their original home near the Black Sea by
the Greeks, the clan of Pheasant was established centuries later in the New World by Euro-Americans. The
birds first lived on estates as domestic fowl, decorative
and symbols of the attainment of goals. The well-to-do
colonists considered Pheasant's kind signs of comfort,
harmony, and satisfaction with life.

The Colonists were not the first people to associate
Pheasant with such lofty ideals and virtues. Nearly every
human population has adopted Pheasant as the sign of

such attainment, embracing him as a natural part of the environment rather than an immigrant. He and his clan have long been admired every where in the world for their positive, spiritual lives as well as their fine plumage and good temper.

Some of Pheasant's tribe prefer the wild life to domestication, and this too, is an expression of attaining goals. Rather than live life as it comes, Pheasant makes the changes needed to live as he pleases, without compromising his comfort or the happiness of his family.

Pheasant lives in attunement with his environment. He works to preserve the surroundings while attaining his goals. He is not the sort of soul who will waste or destroy anything. He lives in harmony, and wishes to leave his children that same harmony. He accepts change as it occurs. He does not court it, to the world's detriment.

Even Ring Necked Pheasant's plumage is a study in harmony. Pleasant to the eye, his fine feathers not only protect him, but ensure him a good mating. Pheasant is an attentive mate and a doting parent.

When Ring Necked Pheasant comes to you, it is to tell you not to neglect hearth and home, comfort and satisfaction. He reminds you that goals set and planned are goals attained. Survival is a matter of living in harmony, working in an environment that is comfortable, to achieve the satisfaction of attaining goals. Waging war to attain your goals is not the same as fighting for what you wish to achieve. It is destructive and creates unhappiness. Fighting for what you want is going out and obtaining the skills, contacts and support you need, while sharing your skills and contacts, and supporting others in their quest.

The reverse of Ring Neck Pheasant's card is to warn that comfort, harmony, satisfaction, and the attainment of goals cannot be achieved at the expense of others, man or beast. You must not exploit the abilities of others, only your own. Are your problems the result of outside forces, or have you contributed to their creation by being self-centered? It is not impossible to stem the tide of wrongness, and work toward the harmony you desperately need.

Chipmunk

VULNERABILITY, POOR PLANNING

Spry and charming, Chipmunk tells of vulnerability and poor planning. This is not because the animal is a poor survivor, but because you need to understand the need to be aware.

Chipmunk comes to counsel that in order to become less vulnerable, you must change your ways and learn to plan. He is a tiny, but industrious, creature, and he is willing to share what he knows. He is legendary when it comes to caching resources, and his dwelling is a study in life-long improvement.

Chipmunk depends on no one for what he needs, though he will share with his friends and family. You do not find him paying a landlord's equity, he owns his house. Nor do you find him living from meal to meal, he has a well-stocked larder because he gets supplies before he buys luxuries.

You must not think Chipmunk spends all of his time worrying and stockpiling. He does not. He works on his house for pleasure as well as planning, but he wants to be sure the house is as safe as possible and should it fail, he can escape.

Are you too dependent on others? Are you failing to conserve some of your resources for the hard times? What causes this in you? Where are the weak points in your psyche and in your environment? What are your escape routes should your plans tumble like a house of cards? Do you have a plan, or is it some vague idea of what you might do if something goes awry?

Always have some sort of plan. Wily chipmunk tells you to always have solid, but flexible, alternatives to any plans you make. Make sure you learn everything you can about what problems you may face, and how to solve those problems should they arise.

Listen to the warning bark and chatter of Chipmunk. He is sounding the warning cry that danger lurks. Beware of the hard times. Those you rely on cannot be relied upon forever. It is not a matter of betrayal or a lack of affection, it is the way of change. Life and luck ebb and flow. You must be prepared, and not be vulnerable. You must plan.

The reverse of this card is a refusal to accept the responsibility of making viable plans, and therefore ensuring your vulnerability. You depend too much on others, while giving them the impression that you need no one's help. It is a dangerous game, and you must shoulder your burden rather than leave it to chance.

Card Patterns and Points

The cards were intended to be aids in problem solving. How the reader chooses to use the cards is, of course, up to the individual. Anyone experienced in the reading of tarot or similar systems can tell you that most of us begin following the recommended systems and then, with dedication, study, and experience, begin creating our own "system".

You will notice in each description there is a definition of the "reverse" of a card. The reverse definitions also contain additional information about the card, its animal and its meanings, so the data is useful whether you use it as a reverse system or not.

It was decided to include the reverse meanings as a matter of tradition, but it is not necessary to use them. These alternate interpretations are primarily used when telling fortunes. When focusing on problems, seeking greater understanding, or requesting spiritual aid, one does not usually lay any card in reverse.

The Totem

It can be very useful to draw an additional card, the Totem, during any reading. The totem is also referred to as a significator card. While the card is usually intended as a totem for the subject during the reading, it will often indicate an important facet of the person's nature and very often the state of that person's psyche at that moment. The totem is never laid in reverse and it is not part of the spread.

There are many card patterns the reader may use. Some are listed here.

The Query

In response to a question, a single card is turned face up. Each successive card adds clarity and detail to the message revealed.

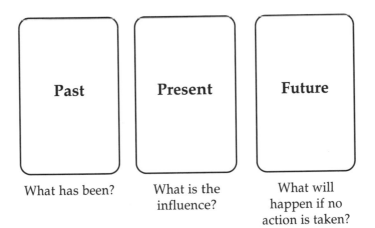

Past

What has been?

Present

What is the influence?

Future

What will happen if no action is taken?

The Wolf Song Spread

Shuffle out the four Wolf cards. Make a cross pattern by placing each wolf at the four compass points as shown in illustration.

Place the remaining cards face down in the center of the cross. Without moving the deck, deal a card to each wolf in North, East, South and West order (step 1). The message of each card may be related to the type of change designated by its corresponding Wolf card (step 2). The understanding and interpretation of the wolves' message will offer insight into your personal situation. The guidance of these animals, with analysis of self and situation, may help you achieve your potential.

North-Timber Wolf

Positive change, natural change. The beginning of the journey to reveal the message. General or preliminary indications of the message.

East-Gray Wolf

Necessary change. Changes which must occur, questions which must be asked or guidance sought to achieve the end result.

South-Red Wolf

Unexpected change. Variables involved or alternatives available.

West-Arctic Wolf

Resistance to change. Obstacles, hesitation or re-evaluation which must be made. The final analysis before the decision is made.

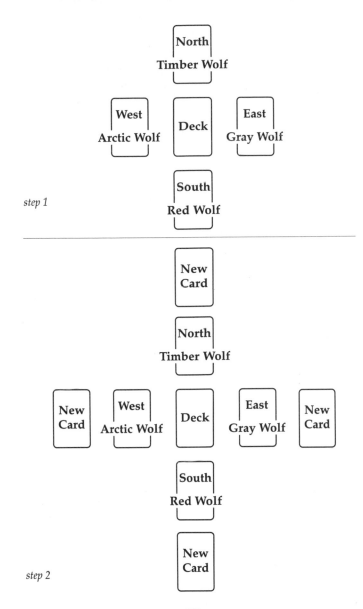

step 1

step 2

165

In Honor of the Kota

Lay four cards to represent North, South, East, and West (step 1). In the spaces that would represent Northeast, Southeast, Northwest and Southwest, place a card (step 2). These represent Grandfather Sky and Grandmother Earth. Beneath the circle, lay seven cards starting at the left and moving to the right (step 3). The first two cards are the past, the second pair are the present, the third set represents the future. The seventh card is the totem and must be head up. The circle above represents the possibilities open to the subject. The line below represents the life as it is now.

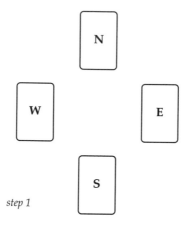

step 1

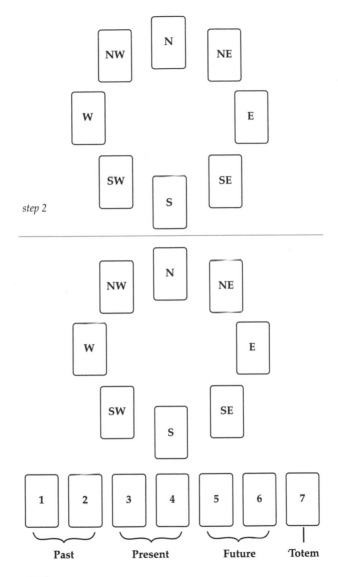

step 2

step 3

General Reading

Lay the cards in three rows, seven cards per row. The top row is the past, the middle row is the present, the last row the future. Draw one card, the totem, and lay it to the bottom of the spread.

Past

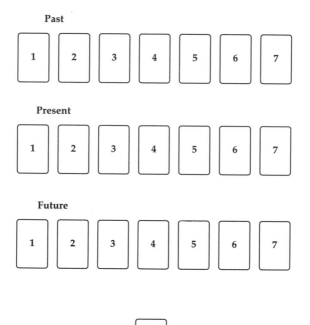

| 1 | 2 | 3 | 4 | 5 | 6 | 7 |

Present

| 1 | 2 | 3 | 4 | 5 | 6 | 7 |

Future

| 1 | 2 | 3 | 4 | 5 | 6 | 7 |

| 7 |

Totem

Yes, No, Maybe

Lay seven cards, left to right. If all the cards are upright, then the answer is a definite yes. If all reverse, then it is no. When the majority of the cards are in one direction and the others in reverse, the answer is maybe. The greater the majority, facing up, the greater the chance of the answer being a good possibility. Example: Four cards upright and three cards reverse means probably yes. Five upright, two reverse, indicate more strength in the probable yes.

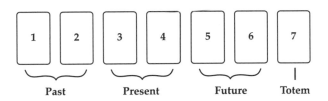

Spirit Cross

This spread uses the entire deck. You begin by aligning the cards in columns from North to South, East to West. Leave a circular space in the center of the compass. Use all but five cards. It does not matter if you pull five from the deck at the beginning or end of the spread, just don't turn them over until you are finished with the cross. Put four of the last five cards at the compass points (N, S, E, W,) to represent the all encompassing Father Sky and Mother Earth. The last card is the totem and it goes in the center of the cross.

It can be useful, as well as very entertaining, to select a totem card for the day. Consider it inspirational or prophetical, as you wish. However you consider it, it will make you think and analyze. That is, after all, the Way of the Wolf, and what the Wolf Song Cards are all about.

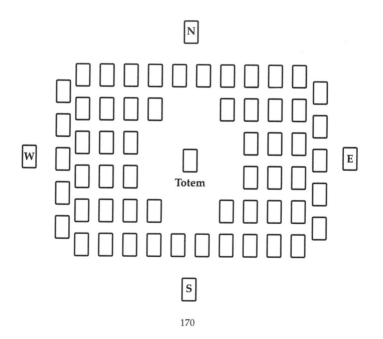

SELECTED BIBLIOGRAPHY

Ahlstrom, Mark E., *The Black Bear*. Ed. Howard Schroeder. Mankato, MN: Baker Street Productions, Crestwood House, 1985.

Ahlstrom Mark E., *The Elk*. Ed. Howard Schroeder. Mankato, MN: Baker Street Productions, Crestwood House, 1985.

Allen, Thomas B., *Vanishing Wildlife of North America*. Washington D.C.: National Geographic, 1974.

Anderson, Robert, *Guide to Florida Mammals*. FL: Erwin Lampert, 1985.

Baer, Donald M., and Elsie M. Pinkston, *Environment & Behavior*. New York: Harper Collins Publishers, 1997.

Bauer, Erwin A., *Wild Dogs: The Wolves, Coyotes and Foxes of North America*. Photographs by Erwin and Peggy Bauer; foreword by John Madson. San Francisco: Chronicle Books, 1994.

Bonners, Susan, *Hunter in the Snow: The Lynx (A Year in the Life of a Female Lynx)*. Boston: Little, Brown, 1994.

Bright, Michael, *Intelligence in Animals*. New York, London: Toucan Books, Reader's Digest Books, 1994.

Burt, William Henry, Illustrations, Richard Philip Grossenheider, *A Field Guide to the Mammals*. Text & Maps: Houghton Mifflin Company. Boston, Cambridge: The Riverside Press, 1964.

Burton, Philip, *Birds of Prey*. Illustrated by Trevor Boyer with Malcolm Ellis and David Thelwell. New York: Gallery Books, 1989.

Busch, Robert H., *The Cougar Almanac: A Complete Natural History of the Mountain Lion*. New York: Lyons & Burford Publishers, 1996.

Carmichal, Peter, and Winston Williams, *Reptiles & Amphibians*. Tampa, FL: World Publications, 1991.

Cassidy, James J., ed., *Through Indian Eyes*. Pleasantville, NY: Reader's Digest Books, 1998.

Cronin, Justin et al., *Atlas of America: Our Nation in Maps, Facts, and Pictures*. New York, Montreal: Reader's Digest, 1998.

Crowell, Pers, *Cavalcade of American Horses*. New York: Bonanza Books, 1951.

Dane, Christopher, *The American Indians and the Occult*. New York: Popular Library (Other Dimension, Inc.), 1973.

DiSilvestro, Roger L., *Fight For Survival*. New York: John Wiley & Sons, Inc., 1990.

Gill, Sam D., and Irene Sullivan, *The Dictionary of Native American Mythology*. Oxford, New York: Oxford University Press, 1992.

Grant, Bruce, *Concise Encyclopedia of the American Indian*. Illustrated by Lorence F. Bjorklund. New York: Bonanza Books, 1960.

Grooms, Steve, *The Return of the Wolf*. Minnetonka, MN: NorthWord Press, Inc., 1993.

Hassrick, Royal B. *The George Catlin Book of American Indians*. New York: Promantory Press, Watson-Guptil, 1977.

Headon, Deidre, *Quest for the Unknown: Man & Beast*. Ed. Tony Whitehorn. New York, London: DK Unlimited, Dorling Kindersley Book, Reader's Digest Books, 1993.

Highwater, Jamake, *The Primal Mind: Vision and Reality in Indian America*. New York: Harper & Row Publishers, Inc., 1981.

Hirschfelder, Arlene, and Martha Kreipe deMontano, *The Native American Almanac*. New York: Prentice Hall, 1997.

Hoage, R.J., ed., *Perceptions of Animals in American Culture*. Washington D.C., London: Smithsonian Institution Press, 1989.

Hoffman, Katherine, *Concepts of Human Identity: Historical and Contemporary Images and Portraits of Self and Family*. New York: Harper Collins, 1996.

Johnston, Johanna, comp., *The Fabulous Fox: An Anthology of Fact & Fiction*. New York: Dodd, Mead, 1979.

Jung, Carl, and M.L. von Franz, Joseph L. Henderson, and Jolande Jacobi, *Man and His Symbols*. Ed. Aniela Jaffe, and Ed. John Freeman. New York: Aldus Books, London, Dell Publising Co., Inc., 1964.

Kaplan, S.R., *Tarot Cards for Fun and Fortune Telling*. Stamford, CT: U.S. Games Systems, Inc., 1970.

Kleiman, Devra G., Mary E. Allen, Katrina V. Thompson, Susan Lumpkin, *Wild Mammals in Captivity*. Ed. Holly Harris. Chicago: University of Chicago Press, 1996.

Kobaleko, Jerry, *Forest Cats of North America: Cougars, Bobcats, Lynx*. Photography by Thomas Kitchin and Victoria Hurst. Ontario: Firefly Books, Willowdale, 1997.

Kroeber, Theodora, *Ishi: In Two Worlds (A Biography of the Last Wild Indian in North America)*. Berkeley and Los Angeles: University of California Press, 1964.

LaFarge, Oliver, *American Indians*. New York: Crown Publishers, Inc., 1964.

Landau, Diane, ed., *Clan of the Wild Cats*. Florence, KT: The Nature Company, Walking Stick Press, 1996.

Lavine, Sigumen A., *Wonders of Foxes*. New York: Dodd, Mead, 1986.

Line, Les J., ed., *The Pleasure of Birds: An Audubon Treasury*. Philadelphia, New York: Lippincott Co. with the Audubon Society, 1975.

Lonsdale, Steven, *Animals and the Origins of Dance*. New York: Thames & Hudson, 1982.

Lopez, Barry Holstun, *Of Wolves and Men*. New York: Charles Scribner's Sons, 1989.

Lowie, Robert H., *Indians of the Plains*. (Originally Published as an Anthropological Handbook by the American Museum of Natural History). New York: American Museum of Natural History, 1954.

Matthiessen, Peter, *Wildlife in America*. New York, Toronto, London: Viking Penguin, Inc., 1987.

McCall, Karen, and Jim Durcher, *Cougar*. Sierra Club, San Francisco, 1992.

McLuhan, T.C., comp., *Touch The Earth: A Self-Portrait of Indian Existence*. London: Abacus Edition, Sphere Books Ltd., 1977.

Mitchell, John Hanson, *A Field Guide to Your Own Back Yard*. New York, London: W.W. Norton & Company, 1985.

Nentl, Jerolyn Ann, *The Wild Cats*. Ed. Howard Schroeder. Mankato, MN: Baker Street Productions, Crestwood House, 1984.

Olson, Dennis L. *Cougars: Solitary Spirits*. Minocqua, WI: NorthWord Press, 1996.

Peterson, Willis, and Eth Clifford. *Wapiti: King of the Woodland*. Photography by Willis Peterson. Chicago: Follett Publishing Co., 1961.

Pough, Richard, *Audubon Land Bird Guide*. New York: Doubleday Nature Guides, 1949.

Propp, V., *Morphology of the Folktale*. Austin, London: Texas Press, 1975.

Savage, Candace, *Eagles of North America*. Ashland, WI: North Word, Inc., 1987.

Smith, Richard P., *Animal Tracks and Signs of North America*. Harrisburg, PA: Stackpole Books, 1987.

Spence, Lewis, *The Myths of the North American Indians*. New York: Dover, 1914.

Spicer; Edward H., *A Short History of the Indians of the United States*. New York: D. Van Norstrand & Co.,1968.

Swinburne, Stephen R., *Once a Wolf: Wildlife Biologists Fought to Bring Back the Gray Wolf*. Photography by Jim Brandenburg. Boston: Houghton Mifflin, 1997.

Taylor, Colin F., and William C. Sturtevant, consults. *The Native Americans: the Indigenous People of North America*. New York: Smithmark, 1996.

Taylor, Colin F., Ph.D., *Plains Indians; A Cultural and Historical View of the North American Plains Tribes of the Pre-Reservation Period*. London: Salamander Books; New Jersey: Random House, 1994.

Thomas, Davis, *People of the First Man: Life Among the Plains Indians in Their Final Days of Glory: The Firsthand Account of Prince Maximilian's Expedition up the Missouri River, 1833-34*. Ed. Karin Ronnefeldt, Watercolors by Karl Bodmer. New York: Promontory Press, E.P. Dutton, from the original account, 1982.

Toops, Connie, *The Enchanting Owl*. Stillwater, MN: Voyageur Wilderness Books, Voyageur Press, 1990.

Vanderwerth, W.C., comp., *Indian Oratory*. New York: Ballantine Books, 1971.

Viola, Herman J., *Seeds of Change: Five Hundred Years Since Columbus*. Ed. Carolyn Margolis. Washington, London: Smithsonian Institution Press, 1991.

Waters, Frank, *Book of the Hopi: the First Revelation of the Hopi's Historical and Religious World View of Life*. Drawings and Source Material Recorded by Oswald White Bear Fredericks. New York: Ballantine Books, 1974.

Weatherford, Jack, From Native *Roots: How the Indians Enriched America*. New York: Crown Publishers, 1991.

Wernert, Susan J., ed., *North American Wildlife*. Pleasantville, NY: Reader's Digest, 1992.

Williams, Winston, *Florida's Fabulous Birds*. Tampa, FL: World Publications, 1986.

Williams, Winston, *Land Birds*. Tampa, FL: World Publications, 1986.

Willis, Roy G., Ph.D., *Man and Beast*. New York, Basic Books, Inc., 1975.

Wood, Daniel, *Bears*. Vancouver: Whitecap Books, 1995.